Building a Successful

and

Ethical Therapy Practice

By

Shaun Brookhouse
GCGI,MA,DCH,PhD,CertEd,PGDHP,DipHyp(Clin),DipProfCouns,HPD,FNGH,FNCH

&

Fiona Biddle
BSc(Hons), DipCAH, Dip Couns, HPD, AccHypSup, CPC, FAPHP, FNCH

UK Academy
of therapeutic arts and sciences

Published by

UK Academy of Therapeutic Arts and Sciences Ltd
16 St Philips Rd, Burton on the Wolds, Loughborough, LE12 5TS
Tel: 01509 881811
Email: info@ukacademy.org
Internet: www.ukacademy.org

ISBN 0-9544604-0-5

Note

Neither the publishers nor the authors will be liable for any loss or damage of any nature occasioned to or suffered by any person acting or refraining from acting as a result of reliance on the material contained in this publication.

Printed in the UK by Lightning Source

Contents

Foreword

It's about time this book was written. There are many good therapists I've had the pleasure of meeting, who despite their skills, struggle to make a living. Many seem to suffer from what you might describe as 'New Age guilt'; that somehow because they are involved in a caring profession they don't deserve to earn a comfortable wage. Interesting that medical consultants don't seem to suffer the same angst! I remember once somebody seeing me after I had taken collection of a new car, taking a look over it and saying "Don't you feel guilty earning money from people's misery?" I smiled and said, "I don't, I earn money from helping people **end** their misery." What is that worth to people? What does that make you worth?

I would further argue that financial solvency assists the quality of your work. If you're sitting with a client and you have a stack of bills piling up in your head, it will affect the clarity of thought you bring to the appointment. Also, I've found that not needing the client to make an appointment when they ring to enquire, increases the number of people who want to – clients respond to exclusivity, but that's hard to project if you really do need them to say yes.

That is why this book is so valuable. There are other books I've read on this topic which give general advice, but the authors of this book this go so much further. The range and depth of advice, coupled with exercises to clarify your outcomes, identify your beliefs and overcome limiting decisions, transforms the book into a business bible, coach and companion. I can imagine that, in the hands of somebody starting out on the rocky road of building a successful practice, their copy will look very dog-eared by the end of the first year – but their business should be thriving!

It says much for the integrity of the authors that they resist a common approach in this field – the 'get rich quick no matter what' theme. As a Hypnotherapist I am regularly inveigled to take trainings that will earn me £100,000 per year working just 2 days per week – and with only 4 days training! Yeh right! My grandfather used to say that the only benefit to doing something easy was that it was easy. Competence takes dedication. Similarly the complementary field is dogged with the miracle 100% guaranteed cure-alls. I'm sure my granddad would have had something to say about that too. Our field has massive potential to do good, and will fulfil that potential when it is filled with people who have pride in their profession, a realistic idea of their capabilities, and a real respect for their clients. If you absorb the advice and values of the authors you will be one of those practitioners.

Enjoy reading this book – that won't be difficult - but please take the action it advises, it will transform your ability to make a living at the thing you love. If the saying is true that "If you do what you love for a living you never work another day in your life," this book could be the route to the most wonderful unemployment!

Trevor Silvester FNCH FHS Cert. Ed HPD NLP Trainer
Author of Wordweaving; The Science of Suggestion

About Us

Shaun Brookhouse has Doctorates in clinical hypnotherapy and education & health services. He also earned Graduateship (First Degree Equivalent) in Counselling and Hypnotherapy and a Masters Degree in Education Studies. Additionally he holds a Cert Ed in Post Compulsory Education. His professional qualifications include diplomas in hypnotherapy from both UK and US institutions. He is a UKCP registered psychotherapist, and a certified professional coach. He also holds a Diploma of Professional Counselling.

Shaun has been the recipient of ten awards within the profession of hypnotherapy including being inducted into the International Hypnosis Hall of Fame and the Rexford L North Memorial Trophy for Life Time Achievement from the National Guild of Hypnotists (the oldest and largest hypnosis society in the world). He is the past chairman of the National Council for Hypnotherapy and was the founding Chair of the UK Confederation of Hypnotherapy Organisations.

He is a fellow of several hypnotherapy and psychotherapy bodies and runs a successful practice and training school in Manchester. He teaches hypnotherapy, NLP, stress management, coaching, counselling and supervision courses. Shaun is the author of "Hypnotherapy Training in the UK", published by Crown House and co-author of Motivational Hypnotism, published by the UK Academy.

Fiona Biddle holds three diplomas in hypnotherapy, a diploma in humanistic counselling and a diploma in transactional analysis. She is also an accredited hypnotherapy supervisor and a certified professional coach. Fiona combines a thriving practice with being the Executive Director of the National Council for Hypnotherapy and runs training courses in coaching, counselling and supervision. Fiona was recipient of the President's Award of the National Guild of Hypnotists, 2004.

*I*ntroduction

This publication is designed to help YOU to be a successful practitioner, while maintaining a high standard of ethical practice. Our aim is to help you to fulfil your potential and indirectly to ensure your clients receive a high quality service.

The book is suitable for practitioners of any complementary therapy including:

Counselling	Acupuncture	Psychotherapy
Hypnotherapy	Meridian Therapies	Osteopathy
Reflexology	Homeopathy	Aromatherapy
Kinesiology	Herbalism	Reiki

The content would also be of use in areas that are not technically therapy, such as life coaching and sports psychology.

We have consulted with practitioners of all the above disciplines to obtain their viewpoints and to ensure that the contents of this publication fit with all their codes of ethics and working practices.

We offer our values, principles and opinions to you in this book. We do not say that you "should" agree with us; there may be ideas within that you find conflict with your values. That is fine: use what fits for you, just please think through your reasons!

Note

We use the word "client" rather than "patient" as some therapies find the use of the latter to suggest an unequal relationship. Others, of course, prefer its use but on balance we decided upon the former.

Elements of a Therapy Practice

In order to have a practice, or indeed any sort of business, there need to be the following elements:

A provider
A service (or product)
A customer

This may seem obvious (and indeed it is), but all these factors are crucial in creating success. You need to work to make yourself the best provider you can possibly be and work to make your service the best it can be. Not only must these two elements be the best, they must also be what the customer wants, and the customer must know they want the benefits you offer.

This is good news! There are lots of areas to work on, and if you do so, you will succeed. However, there are many therapists who dislike that word "work". They may be happy to do their therapy, but not be keen on the other bits. We aim to show you that these other bits can be just as interesting (if not more so sometimes), and their benefit will be immense.

The following chapters in this publication will give you many ideas on how to achieve these aims. We can break the elements down further to:

Being the best therapist you can be
Providing the best service you can
Letting your clients know you are there
Letting your clients know they need you

Therefore we will cover the standard issues of how and where to advertise, but this publication goes much further than this, to give you the full package to excellence and success.

Income Formula

Let us introduce you to the first of our formulae. This was created by the authors to illustrate the elements that seem to contribute to the amount of income that is received by anyone undertaking any role.

There may well be exceptions to this rule but we have not, as yet, found any.

Income = value ×
difficulty ×
rarity ×
image ×
number of users

The "number of users" element of the formula needs an explanation immediately as this may not be obvious. By this we mean someone who benefits from what the provider does. This may be direct or indirect. For example a best selling novelist will have millions of users who benefit from their work, while a surgeon will have few users as it is normal to operate on only one person at a time.

To illustrate this formula let's look at some examples:

H=High, M=Medium, L=Low

	Value	Difficulty	Rarity	Image	N Users	Income
David Beckham	H	H	H	H	H	H++++
Plumber	H	M	M	M	L	M
Nurse	M	M	M	L	L	L
Cleaner	L	L	L	L	L	L

To explain, the <u>perceived</u> value of what Beckham does for his "users" is high, as is that of the plumber (you really need that washing machine!). Beckham might not find what he does difficult but most would, and few are so good at it. There are things which are rare but not difficult (eg being a sagger maker's bottom knocker), or difficult but not rare (eg counselling).

Image comes into the equation too. There are other footballers with the same level of skill etc. as Beckham, but without the glamour. They might come in at M or L on image and the resulting income would be that much lower.

The image of the role itself is also a factor. For example, it could be argued that the actual work done by an air steward is very similar to that of a waitress, but one has a much higher image than the other.

Help your client see that your therapy is as valuable as gold

Finally the number of users impacts greatly on income. Take the example of the nurse. A nurse can only look after so many people at one time, and this limits the income dramatically, whereas David Beckham's skills are enjoyed by millions.

So, how does this affect you in your role as therapist? Simply that you have the opportunity to work to maximise each element of the formula. Different therapies will have different challenges. For example, maximising the "N users" element might be possible for those who can do group sessions. Even an osteopath can have more than one client on the go at once if one is receiving heat treatment for example while another is being manipulated.

However, you may prefer to work one to one and not too many hours, and so concentrate your efforts on the other elements. The image of different therapies will vary, but there is always the opportunity to work on this through the way you behave and market yourself.

And remember, most of these elements are perceptions, and it is the perceptions of your "users" that need to be maximised. It can be very useful to ask friends and colleagues about their perceptions of all these factors, and of you too, if you dare!

The exercise that follows can be repeated at regular intervals to see your progress.

Income Formula Exercise

How would your potential clients rate **your** therapy practice on the following elements?

value   _____

difficulty   _____

rarity   _____

image   _____

How would you rate your therapy practice on the following?

number of users   _____

Which of the above need to be worked on?

How, specifically, are you going to do this?

When are you going to do this?

How will you know when you have succeeded?

The Success Formula

Another formula (the last for a while, at least). This is designed (again by the authors) to show the elements required in a process to have a successful outcome:

$$Success = goal + movement + resources - obstacles$$

If we use a football analogy, success (scoring), requires a goal (literally), movement of the player, resources (ie a ball) and an absence of obstacles (ie players of the other team) OR getting round the obstacles.

In terms of therapy, let's look at each of these elements:

Goal: if you don't know where you are going, you probably won't get there. Therefore you need to set targets. What does success mean to you in the short and long term?

Movement: that means you doing things, taking action and not just sitting, waiting for clients to drop metaphorically into your lap.

Resources: things such as this manual, the Internet, journals, colleagues, and professional societies, all of which can assist you in achieving success

Obstacles: these can be internal or external. For example, fear of success and lack of knowledge are internal obstacles, and lots of competition and inappropriate premises are external obstacles.

Let's look at goals, resources and obstacles in more depth. (Movement is covered throughout this manual)

Goal

In order to get what you want, you must know what you want

Ok, so it's not always true: Fiona didn't know she wanted a digital camera until she won one in a competition, but conversely, she would never have got to the position of writing this book if she hadn't known she wanted to.

You may have only a vague idea of what you want and need. Your ideas may be abstract, precise or anywhere in between. That is ok, for now, but let's look at how to bring clarity to your aims: the process is to get you to the specifics, and then for you to find routes to achieve the aims.

The Process:

It is important to start from where you are now. (This doesn't exclude looking for causes as to why you are at this point. If you find that this is a need you have, then see section on therapy under Maintaining Standards, p149)

The exercise on p19 will help you to analyse your

- Needs
- Wants
- Desires
- Ambitions

From this you will discover (if you don't already know) what success means to you. This exercise can be used in conjunction with the values exercise on p51. It is important to tie in all elements of you, your life and your practice to develop a congruent whole. This also means analysing areas of your life other than your practice, so feel free to use these exercises to set goals for areas such as relationships, family, health, fitness, personal growth and spirituality as well as your career. Deciding what you want in life involves different levels. It can be helpful when thinking of goals to consider the big picture first and to contemplate your overall position in the world.

Chunking down

In this exercise you will be asked to "chunk down". This means getting from a high level of abstraction to low. High levels are ideas such as Happiness, Fulfilment, or Success. These are, of course, fine as goals, but we "chunk down" to find out what they really mean, and it is important to recognise that what they mean to you may well be different to what they mean to anyone else.

Here is an example of a coach using this technique with a client to discover a goal.

Coach's Questions	Response
What do you want?	Freedom
	↓
What would you need in order to have freedom, specifically?	
	Money
	↓
How much money?	
	Enough money to do what I want
What specifically?	↓
	Provide the family with 'little extras'
Specifically?	↓
	Holidays and a Jacuzzi
How much do you need, per year to do this?	↓
	An extra £8,000

So now the coach and the client know what the client wants, specifically, and together they can move on to look at how to achieve the goal and to break this down into small measurable steps and actions to take to move in this direction.

Goals should be:

- small rather than large
- concrete, specific, behavioural
- the start of something, not the end
- positive indicators of success, not the absence of problems
- realistic and achievable
- realistically achievable: break them down to short timescales (eg two weeks)
- involving work, as perceived by the client and/or family

When the goals have been set it is vital they should be written down. Drawing can also help, as can creating scrapbooks. But however they are put onto paper they must then be used, not just hidden in a draw.

Goals should be reviewed daily, without fail!

Seeing the big picture

Types of Goals

The basic motivations in life are avoidance of pain and pursuit of pleasure. All goals can be chunked up to this ultimately. Research has shown that the motivation to avoid pain is more than twice as strong as the motivation towards pleasure. In developing your marketing strategies, you will need to take this factor into account.

Motivation also needs energy and the energy to take action needs to be stronger than the energy required to stay still.

Goals can also be divided into two types, called Means and Ends. Means defines a goal that involves a process, Ends are goals that concentrate on a specific result.

Eg:

Away from/Means:	to avoid workplace confrontation
Away from/Ends	to avoid dying from heart disease
Towards/Means	to get a sun tan
Towards/Ends	to feel happy

Next time you are watching television, pay attention to the adverts and see what motivators they are using to sell their products.

Goal Setting Exercise

For questions 1-4 below write with little thought, as many things as you can think of.

1. What do you want?

2. What do you need?

3. What do you desire?

4. What ambitions do you have?

Read through what you have written and pick out the ONE THING that stands out the most.

Chunk this down (as shown on page 16), using the table on the next page to help you.

Repeat with some or all of the other answers you have produced above. You may well find you start getting repetitive goals.

Create a plan for each goal, using the chart on p21, and make sure to review all goals DAILY.

	GOAL
	Write your original need/want/desire/ambition here
What does this mean to you, specifically?	
And what would you need to have this?	
More specifically?	
More specifically?	
More specifically?	
More specifically?	
More specifically?	
More specifically?	

GOAL:

Target date for reaching goal:

	Steps	Date	Done
1			
2			
3			
4			
5			
6			
7			
8			

Resources

There are lots of things that you can use to help you in your practice. Below is a list of some possibilities for you.

- Books about your subject
- Books about related subjects
- Books about running a business
- Self-help books
- Your own therapy
- Other types of therapy
- Other professions
- Tapes
- CDs
- Videos
- Research databases
- Journals
- Libraries
- The Internet
- Professional bodies
- Special interest groups
- Colleagues
- Your supervisor (see p147)
- A mentor
- A coach
- Local business groups
- Your experience
- Your skills
- Your knowledge
- Your aptitudes
- Your attitudes
- Friends
- Family
- Local colleges/universities

Resources Exercise

Go through the list on the previous page, and for each item, make a list of

1. What you already have in this category that can help you

2. Anything in this category that is a problem, and for each problem find a strategy to reframe (see p157) or reduce the impact of the problem

3. What, specifically you need more of in this category and how you can get it.

4. Action you are going to take in relation to this item.

Review this exercise on a regular basis: feel resourced!

Support

Being a therapist can be a lonely business. This may seem strange in that you are constantly in contact with people, but as we will discuss in the section of this book on the relationship between therapist and client, the contact, while real, is not designed to fulfil your needs.

Therapy can be a lonely place

It is important for you to set up a network of contacts who you can turn to as necessary for any of the following:

- Professional support
- Professional advice
- Referring on
- Offloading
- Friendship

These are likely to be different people as it is important that boundaries do not get muddled. For example, if your therapy is one which uses supervision then you will know that the supervisory relationship, while being friendly, is not friendship.

Professional advice may represent many different areas such as advice on:

- Your own therapy
- Related therapies
- Legal matters
- Financial matters
- Medical matters
- Ethical issues

Support Exercise

Use the table below to list the types of support you need or may need (ideas in grey), and list names of the people you can approach:

Type of Support	Names
Professional (eg supervision)	
Advice on my therapy	
Advice on other therapies	
Legal advice	
Financial	
Medical advice	
Ethical advice	
Referring on	
Offloading	
Friendship	

Obstacles

Often simply an awareness that an obstacle is there can shrink it. They often take on unrealistic proportions until analysed.

Obstacles can be REMOVED, gone OVER, UNDER, AROUND or THROUGH, SHRUNK, or UTILISED.

A novel way of getting THROUGH an obstacle

Here are some examples:

- A newly qualified counsellor cannot find suitable premises from which to work, so she gets AROUND this by converting her dining room into a consulting room.

- A change to the code of ethics means that Bob feels unable to continue in practice. He gets OVER this obstacle by retraining.

- Holly feels that she cannot deal with clients with a particular problem as she has it too, but realises that with assistance from her own therapist and supervisor, she can UTILISE her own experience to make her particularly effective with these clients.

- Mark has let his fear of success hinder his progress in setting up his practice. He REMOVES this obstacle through therapy.

- Donna has two children and a third on the way. Her business is suffering as she has so little time to devote to it. This problem is SHRUNK by effective time management.

- Joe has cut corners on his marketing and missed out on this year's Yellow Pages. On realising his mistake, he gets UNDER the obstacle by ascertaining other places to advertise, and invests in those.

- Two therapists with the same training as Anne set up in her small town. She gets THROUGH this obstacle by working with them so that they all know who has which strengths for referring, and they set up a programme of workshops between them.

Obstacles Exercise

Use this chart to analyse any obstacles that you perceive to your success. Be wild and wacky: you can always discard ideas later.

	Write your obstacle here
How could I get OVER it?	
How could I REMOVE it?	
How could I get THROUGH it?	
How could I get UNDER it?	
How could I SHRINK it?	
How could I get AROUND it?	
How could I UTILISE it?	

*B*eing the Best Therapist You Can Be

In the description of the elements of a therapy practice, we highlighted the need to

Be the best therapist you can be

We will look at this element in more detail here. Therapies vary in terms of how much freedom the therapist has in terms of the treatment they offer. Some therapies are more formulaic or mechanistic than others, but we would argue that in all of them, the contribution of the therapist to the therapy is a vital factor.

For example, reflexologists may be taught a specific set of techniques and the order in which these techniques are applied, but they are not robots, and the manner in which the client is dealt with, before, during and after their session will impact greatly on its perceived success. It is interesting to compare this with allopathic medicine, where we all understand the relevance of the "bedside manner". But there are cases where the doctor has no relationship with the patient at all. One of the authors had the experience of having an operation and being visited the next day on a ward round, and on asking who had performed the operation, none of the doctors present could remember whether it was them or not!

In all therapies the therapist offers

- Their skills and knowledge
- A relationship

The Relationship

How much attention is paid to the relationship between therapist and client varies greatly depending on the therapy offered and the training involved. For example, in hypnotherapy, some training courses, and many of the books simply say that "rapport is needed", without defining rapport, let alone explaining how to "get it".

Therapy is a profession which involves interaction with people. Being a therapist means adopting a role while your client adopts a corresponding role. Therapists brings aspects of themselves into the role, ie they are real people interacting with other real people.

The paragraph above may appear to be stating the obvious, but this is of crucial importance to the success of therapy and therefore your success as a therapist.

The importance of connection

We believe the relationship that is created between you, the therapist, and your client is one of the most significant factors in your success. Can you think of any profession that involves interaction between people that is not aided by good interpersonal skills? We have all seen examples of those who do not see it as important:, the patronising doctor, the authoritarian teacher, the bullying policeman, but what is really needed is CONTACT. Contact between one human being and another. One understanding the other and showing that understanding.

Creating a relationship based on honesty, truth, trust and acceptance is so powerful it almost defies words. But this must be your aim, with each and every client or potential client.

The therapist is responsible for building this relationship. By offering this, clients can respond and find themselves in a position where they can accept all that you are offering them. The building of the relationship starts with their very first contact with you, whether in person, through your advertising, or through a third party. All of these factors need to create the right start, which can then be built on by your interactions.

Let us look at some basic facts about therapy that you may or may not agree with:

- Clients want to be listened to
- Clients want to be valued
- Clients want their therapist to be honest with them
- Clients want to be allowed to be themselves
- Clients do not want to be judged
- Clients want their therapist to be a real person
- Clients want to make their own choices

If you agree with these statements then you probably have a leaning towards humanistic principles. Many people have, but many of them don't realise it. Often the authors have asked a class whether they are humanistic to be greeted with blank expressions. On explanation the enthusiasm often follows.

Humanistic Principles

- People have free will and can make their own choices
- People are capable of change and strive to fulfil potential
- People are more than just their behaviour
- Scientific laws do not describe everything that is human
- People are consciously aware of their existence and can reflect, change and participate in their existence
- People create their own meaning from their own experience; everyone's perception is their own

Not all therapists are humanistic, and that is fine (being humanistic allows others the choice not to be.). We include this section for your interest due to our awareness that many find this to be useful ground for their work.

Probably the most common definition of the therapeutic relationship comes from the work of Carl Rogers that led to the development of person-centred counselling. Below we outline the main points from this view of the relationship. Doubtless elements will vary depending on the therapy offered, but the fundamental points will hold true for any therapeutic relationship.

Core conditions

In all therapeutic relationships, there is a need for the client to feel safe. The client needs to trust the therapist, as the client needs to know that the therapist has their best interests at heart. This trust can best be developed by creating a relationship based on the Rogerian Core Conditions.

These conditions are often misinterpreted, as they have been adapted by the client-centred counselling theorists to sometimes an extreme stance of a lack of challenge. In some therapy roles, however, challenge can be very much a part of the work. But this can be done from the angle of the core conditions. The core conditions are;

Empathy

"Empathy is the ability to perceive the internal frame of reference of another with accuracy, and with the emotional components and meanings which pertain thereto, as if one were the other person, but without ever losing the 'as if' condition. Thus it means to sense the hurt or the pleasure of another as he senses it, and to perceive the causes thereof as he perceives them, but without ever losing the recognition that it is as if I were hurt or pleased etc. If this 'as if' quality is lost, then the state is one of identification."

Carl Rogers (1959)

OR:

The ability to

- grasp the subjective world of another
- try to be in another's shoes
- understand that their background have caused these ways of being
- recognise that you do not know everything about them

THIS SHOWS:

- understanding
- acceptance
- not being judged

Unconditional Positive Regard

"When the therapist is experiencing a warm, positive and acceptant attitude toward what *is* in the client, this facilitates change. It involves the therapist's genuine willingness for the client to be whatever feeling is going on in him at that moment, - fear, confusion, pain, pride, anger, hatred, love, courage, or awe. It means that the therapist cares for the client, in a non-possessive way. It means that he prizes the client in a total rather than a conditional way. By this I mean that he does not simply accept the client when he is behaving in certain ways, and disapprove of him when he behaves in other ways. It means an outgoing positive feeling without reservations, without evaluations. The term we have come to use for this is unconditional positive regard. Again research studies show that the more this attitude is experienced by the therapist, the more likelihood there is that therapy will be successful."

Carl Rogers (1961)

It is often difficult to feel unconditional positive regard, particularly when a client's behaviour does not fit with your value system. However, as a therapist it is not your job to judge your client, so it helps to remember that you can disapprove of behaviour while still recognising that the person is still a human being who is inherently worthy of being valued.

If you cannot feel this for a particular client it would be unethical to take them on so refer to a colleague. It may be that there is a particular category of client or issue that you are unable to work with. Be clear within yourself as to your limits and stay within them. It may be that with work you can make changes within yourself to remove the barrier or you may choose not to, but whatever happens you need always to be clear about who you are comfortable to work with (or not) and why.

Congruence

Congruence has been also described as realness, authenticity or genuineness. This means therapists being who they are, being honest with themselves and the client. This depends on the therapists' capacities for knowing both themselves and their subject. Without either of these being fully developed, the therapist will not be perceived as being congruent, and as with the other core conditions it is the client's perception of it that matters most.

If the client sees the therapist as being a real person, they can feel more secure in being one too, which means they will feel more comfortable in showing what might otherwise be perceived as weaknesses. It is important, however that therapists remain fully aware that their presence in the relationship is to serve the client and so must not use the theory of congruence as an excuse to get their own needs met by sharing too much with their clients.

Achieving empathy, congruence & unconditional positive regard

To achieve empathy, acceptance, realness and create a safe place for the client, a therapist needs:

* An ability to be involved whilst also detached, to be outside as well as inside.
* To have their own feelings/opinions but keep them out of the session.
* To focus on the client, rather than the therapists's own needs/views.
* To judge behaviour rather than the person (and refer them on if cannot).
* To show respect at all levels, including keeping time, quality of room, and giving full attention.
* To be aware of own bias, blocks etc and work with these.
* To be prepared to look at what is raised in themselves by the client..
     what do they tell you about your self.. who do they remind you of.?
* To be committed to growth and professionalism
* To be open and receptive.
* To use intuition but always check it out.
* Never to over-step empathy by invasion. The client has the choice of how far to let you in.
* To stay congruent: with self (by owning own views and feelings) and with the client (by owning response to their behaviour and not blaming.)
* Not to collude.
* To use 'responsibility language' ..'I' statements and acknowledgement of choices.
* To maintain own boundaries and empowering the client to have their own.
* To explore why the client is behaving/feeling as they do.

In these ways the therapist establishes rapport with the client and builds a relationship based on understanding the other person.

How much it is appropriate for clients to tell you about themselves will depend on the therapy you offer. If you are a counsellor for example, the client needs to know that there is nothing that cannot be discussed. By creating this environment you are enabling the client to feel safe to share and explore anything. If however, you feel it inappropriate for your client to divulge personal information that is not relevant to your therapy, then it is a vital part of the relationship that you find a way to convey this to your clients without them feeling rejected.

Further Reading Recommendations:

Person Centred Counselling in Action: Mearns & Thorne
The authors of this course have differing opinions on the value of person-centred counselling due to very different experiences of this. However, whatever its value as a therapy in its own right, this book gives an excellent introduction to the concepts of creating a therapeutic alliance, which translates very well to being used in the coach/client relationship.

The Reality Game: John Rowan
This book is an introduction to humanistic counselling and once again gives a good insight into the basics of creating rapport and how this affects the process of change.

50 Ways to Get Along with Absolutely Everyone: Chuck Spezzano
If you can get beyond the rather tacky title, some of the content is excellent and enlightening.

Relationship Exercise

This is an exercise that you can complete for any or all clients on a regular or occasional basis, as you choose.

Ask yourself the following questions and be as honest with yourself as you can. Ensure that these notes adhere to the criteria for confidentiality and note taking in the Ethics chapter.

Client   _____

1. In what areas is it hard to be empathic with this client?

2. Have I demonstrated empathy adequately to this client? How could I have improved?

3. Have I judged this client? Negatively or positively. Have I shown any such judgements?

4. Have I demonstrated my congruence?

5. Have I avoided talking about myself too much? Have I kept my own process out of the relationship?

Needs

Everyone has needs and it could be argued that everything that anyone does is designed to fulfil a need at some level. If you agree with this premise then it becomes clear that working as a therapist is fulfilling one or more need for you; needs which may be appropriately filled in this way, or not.

In this area, as in so many others, there are differences of opinion. Perhaps this can be seen as a continuum with completely fine at one end to downright unethical at the other. Professional societies and governing bodies are responsible for defining some positioning, but there will be some decisions that you will need to make for yourself.

You are not your client's parent

Needs Exercise

Use this exercise to become clear as to which of your needs you are seeking to fill through your work.

For each potential need listed, decide how big a factor it is for you, and then decide whether this ethically acceptable, whether it leads to you behaving inappropriately and whether it would be of benefit to seek to fulfil this need elsewhere.

Be honest and give these questions a lot of thought. Glib answers will help no one!

How reliant on client income are you for survival?

Do your clients make you feel useful or needed?

Do you consciously or unconsciously mother/father your clients?

Do you get a feeling of power from your work?

Does your position give you a feeling of status?

Do you need to demonstrate your competence?

Do you get a feeling of relatedness through your client work?

Are you seeking to deal with your own issues through your work?

Are you seeking to block your own feelings through your work?

Collusion

When you find yourself getting caught up in agreeing with the client, being fascinated by the content and asking questions for you own interest, making comments on the other people and the situation; then you are communicating a judgement and may well be colluding with them. This is different from having positive regard which means communicating your acceptance and valuing of the client without judgement.

In a typical counselling relationship, collusion is comparatively easy to avoid; in coaching it is trickier as one of the coach's main roles is to be the client's biggest fan, motivator and supporter!

So the tricky part is to do this without colluding, for the problems detailed below can still occur.

Examples of collusion:
"That sounds awful for you"
"how upsetting"
"so he made you feel angry"
laughing with them when it wasn't funny
"Oh I know"
"Yes people are so.........."
"So there was nothing you could do about it"
"How uncaring of her"

Why might we do it?
Feeling sympathy, it's easier, because the client is manipulating us, to avoid confrontation, to rescue, for our own needs (eg to be liked, in control), through boredom, through wanting to get results.

When you notice yourself doing this, or feel the impulse to do it then:
-Use empathy as a focus, NOT sympathy, getting into their experience alone, helps keep YOU out of it.

-If the CONTENT is interesting, ask how they feel about it or keep paraphrasing. This moves into PROCESS and gets away from your connection to the content.

-Remember you do not know any one else in the story and don't know their experience so don't pass comment on them, reflect back that this is your client's experience of these people/the situation.

-Keep boundaries. You care but are not involved.

Collusion won't help your client's well-being

Beliefs and Values

Beliefs

We all have a huge number of beliefs about ourselves and the world. It can be difficult to draw the line between a fact and a belief. This is one of the most important lessons to learn as a therapist, because crucially, your beliefs and opinions will not be the same as your clients', but they will definitely and significantly affect the way that you are as a therapist, the service you offer and the perception your clients have of you.

These beliefs will be underpinning all your work with the client, right from what might be considered to be trivial beliefs (eg one should dress smartly for work) through to beliefs about yourself (eg I am not clever enough to succeed), through to beliefs about other people (eg men are all untrustworthy), through to beliefs about society (eg religion is the source of all the world's problems).

Many of these beliefs are likely to have been swallowed whole from someone else, usually a parent, school or society. In Gestalt terms this process is called introjection. As children we are all given messages about who and what we are and should be. These messages, to a greater or lesser extent, help to form our sense of self.

Clients will often "show" their introjects by the use of "I am" or "I should" statements. How relevant this process is to you will depend on what sort of therapy you offer. Here we are more interested in YOUR introjects and how they affect the process as outlined on p 6 (Elements of a Therapy Practice).

Here are some examples of personal introjects:

- I am untidy however hard I try
- I am never going to amount to much
- I am better than people of a different race
- I am hopeless at maths
- I am too sensitive

Here are some examples of "shoulds". Be aware of how many of these can get in the way of making progress:

- I should change
- I shouldn't feel like this
- It's all my fault
- I should do better
- I should be slimmer/fitter/more like my mother/better
- I shouldn't complain

If you can acknowledge and accept the reality of where you are and choose change if required, you are halfway there.

Labels are a special case of limiting beliefs. As soon as a label has stuck, it is difficult to remove. Here are some such labels:

Stupid	Clumsy	Depressed	Careless
Good girl/boy	Eccentric	Bonkers	Loser
Scruffy	A joke	Rude	Womaniser
Delicate	Funny	Gregarious	Paranoid
Clever	Wimp	Shy	Polite

As you can see, some of these may be perceived as positive, but these can be just as limiting as the negative labels.

So, challenge your own beliefs, gently and carefully, making sure you feel safe to explore your true feelings and to re-evaluate. A process that lasts a lifetime. If necessary get help with the process by seeking a well qualified therapist who could help you in your exploration. In some therapies a supervisor might also be able to assist you with this process.

"I can't believe that" said Alice

"Can't you?" said the Queen in a pitying tone. "Try again. Draw a long breath and shut your eyes."

Alice laughed.

"There's no use trying." She said. "One can't believe impossible things."

"I daresay you haven't had much practice," said the Queen. "When I was your age, I always did it for half an hour a day. Why sometimes I believed six impossible things before breakfast."

Lewis Carrol
Alice in Wonderland

Here are some typical beliefs that get in the way of progress:

- Putting others first
- Being too old or too young
- Not enough money
- Too many commitments
- Belief in fate
- Following material goals
- Feeling of not being deserving

Beliefs Exercise: Self

Rate yourself on the following traits on a scale of 1 to 5, where 1 is not at all and 5 is very much so. JUST DO IT: QUICKLY.

Good		Odd	
Kind		Distant	
Tidy		Selfish	
Stupid		Tough	
Shy		Daft	
Poor at concentrating		Sad	
Caring		Lovely	
Weak		Messy	
Creative		Interested	
Masculine		Extroverted	
Naughty		Dull	
Happy		Clever	
Cool		Friendly	
Normal		Feminine	
Sensitive		Cruel	
Punctual		Strong	
Passionate		Attentive	
Arrogant		Funny	
Conservative		Musical	
Interesting		Committed	

Now, go through and see which of these are REALLY you, which you have believed you were, but could choose not to be, or which you have believed you couldn't be, but could.

Look at how you perceive these qualities. You may see a quality as negative when others (maybe from a different culture) would see it as positive. What do YOU feel?

Also, look at those to which you give a value judgement, and see what options you have, look at those things you fear being, and finally ask other people how they see you: it may be very different.

Beliefs Exercise: the World

Finish these phrases with the first thing to come into your head: thought is not allowed.

Men are
Most people are
Religion is
Politicians are
Women are
Getting old is
People should always
Mothers are
Working hard is
Children are
Voting conservative is
Qualifications are
Clothes are
Belief in God is
Trusting others is
Being safe means
Food is
Fathers are
Doing nothing is
Love is

Now review your answers and compare them with the beliefs you were brought up with, both at home and school. How much are these your ideas, and how much are they introjected?

Values

Values are what we believe to be important. These are the ideals to which we subscribe. Values are also one of the filtering criteria that we use to codify the world.

When looking at values, we need to look at how our values are formed. Many of us will remember when we were told right from wrong as children. As children we were instilled with a certain set of beliefs and values which still forms the cornerstone of our identity today.

As therapists when we look at what is important to us, we probably value things like:

- Helping people
- Transformation
- Empathy
- Satisfaction in life

The interesting part of looking at one's values is that when we ask "What is important to you about being a therapist?" the first answer is often the answer that one expects to get, ie. "I want to help people. This, of course, is laudable, and it is interesting to note, that financial security or compensation often does not even make the list. One reason for this is that financial compensation is often pooh-poohed by therapeutic trainers and societies because of the belief that therapy is a vocation rather than a profession.

If we are not appropriately compensated for our work, despite the fact that we may want to help people, we will not be in practice long enough to help anyone at all because we cannot pay the bills. We mention this because when it comes to looking at the things that we value in life, we need to be honest with ourselves, rather than just saying what we think we should or what other people expect of what we say.

In our experience we have found that the people who do not succeed in therapy are not bad therapists. In fact, many excellent therapists fail to survive more than a few months in practice. This is not because of a lack of skill, but rather a lack of value in themselves. When we work with clients we need to employ the core conditions to ourselves as well as our clients. When clients value themselves as well as their clients they provide a model of excellence from which their clients can get great benefit.

Your client's values may be very different to yours

Values Exercise

Pick out the top 10 things that are important to you about being a therapist. Do not codify them at first just brainstorm. When you have your 10 rate them on a scale of 1-10 and see what you find. Then, rank these values in priority order. You may be surprised as to what is really important to you about being a therapist.

Rank in Priority Order	Value/Description	Score Level of Satisfaction Scale of 1 to 10 (10 = Highest)

Who and what are you?

By now, we are sure you are getting a good idea of where we are going with these ideas:

You need to know who and what you are, feel confident in being you and value yourself in order to make a success of your therapy practice.

In the Beliefs and Values exercises you have been examining aspects of yourself, now let's look at aspects of yourself specifically related to your offering of a therapy service.

The exercise that follows will help you to rate yourself on the different aspects of your particular therapy, but it is likely that you will need skills in all the following areas, as well as those specific to your therapy:

- Building a relationship
- Business practice
- Legal and ethical issues
- Anatomy and physiology

We have covered the first of these already and we will look at the second and third in general terms later. We will not be looking at A & P: there are plenty of sources for you to learn this if your knowledge is lacking. The point is that you need to be good at everything, but the good news is that you can. The hard part is YOUR therapy, and that you are trained in (aren't you?)

We talked earlier about how labels can be limiting, but the following, if you get to the point where they really are about YOU, can be empowering:

So are you:

Ethical ?	Qualified ?	Skilled ?	An expert ?
Open ?	Committed ?	Aware ?	Knowledgeable ?
Positive ?	Determined ?	Thorough ?	Still learning ?

If so, you have what it takes to be successful!

Me and My Therapy

Rate yourself on the following elements on a scale of 1 to 5, where 1 is unskilled and 5 is expert.

Empathy	
Unconditional Positive Regard	
Congruence	
Business practice	
Legal issues	
Ethics	
Anatomy and Physiology	
Write in specific skills for your therapy in the remaining lines	

Are you happy with your scores? Do they help to give you the labels as shown on the previous page? How can your scores be improved? What do you need to do?

Appearance

Unfortunately there is no getting away from the fact that appearance matters. How you look will be influence others' perception of who and what you are. Some of their conclusions will be in their conscious awareness, but at other times people will be unaware that they are, in effect, judging you.

The authors were recently at a seminar during which the presenter made some very specific claims as to how one "should" appear as a therapist, including having no facial hair, no jewellery other than a wedding ring, and not wearing a hairpiece as this was a sign of insecurity. We would not choose to take such a strong stance; all we suggest is that you consider your choices about how you present yourself to the world and look at your reasons for your choices.

There are specific things that clients are likely to expect when they see you for the first time, and whether you conform to their expectations is a matter for your choice. One of the authors remembers a fellow student once saying that you should dress appropriately for each client, which conjured up an image of a Mr Benn type changing room.

Our suggestions would be that you

- Are always clean
- Dress comfortably
- Choose somewhere in the middle of the relaxed/formal continuum of clothing
- Do not attempt to "impress" your clients by your chosen style of appearance. For example, if your branch of therapy would lend itself to wearing a white coat then do, otherwise do not.
- Always appear professional. No slippers, cigarettes, or cut off jeans!

Credibility

Throughout this book we are inherently referring to your need to appear credible to your potential clients. The best way to do this is to know your stuff, know yourself, and develop the skills to demonstrate these things to your potential and current clients.

The authors have read a recent article on credibility which listed a range of people that the author of the article felt showed such great credibility that they almost defined the word. Unfortunately one or two in the list just caused us to laugh. This was an excellent demonstration of the difference in perception. One person may perceive another as credible whereas another may not.

So what can you do to maximise your credibility for the maximum number of people? Enhance your skills in demonstrating:

- Competence
- Empathy
- A balance between humility and arrogance
- Confidence
- Professionalism

You need to bear in mind who you are aiming your services at and adjust your approach accordingly. For example you will need to adjust your language appropriately. Let's say you are a homeopath with clients all of whom are suffering from bladder problems. One is a GP, another a 5 year old, and the third is a 20 year old soldier. We don't think we need to tell you in which case you would be best to use the word wee-wee, when to opt for urinate, or when to choose pee?

Getting these things wrong loses you credibility so quickly. You may be perceived as ignorant or arrogant, when you need to be seen as on their wavelength but knowledgeable. Being congruent and showing this, helps build credibility. It can help to show that you are human, and showing minor flaws will aid this process too. For example, one can, if applicable, disclose that you had similar issues at one time of your life, and that you have overcome them, but still occasionally have your battles with it. By doing this you show that you have been there, and that it is okay to occasionally have to revisit the issue even after one has "got over it".

Modelling

Modelling is a formalised process of ascertaining what makes excellent people excellent at what they do. In the early 1970's Richard Bandler and John Grinder, set out to model key therapists who seemed to achieve consistently good results with clients, even in cases where traditional means of treatment have failed. This project was to form the basis of what is known today as Neuro Linguistic Programming.

The most important component to modelling is curiosity. If one wants to find and even become a model of excellence one must be curious about oneself, as well as the person(s) one is modelling. Modelling is different to copying. Copying is a simplistic process where one does what someone else does without understanding the motives or reasons why. Modelling attempts to give the modeller insight into why the model does what he or she does and thereby giving modellers the choice in what behaviours they may want to integrate in themselves.

There are three components that modellers look at when it comes to modelling: Beliefs/Values, Strategies and Behaviour Integration. We have already looked at beliefs and values earlier in this text. We shall now look at the other two components.

Strategies

Strategies, simply put, are the processes that a person undertakes to achieve a certain result. In NLP, we refer to the TOTE Model of Strategies. TOTE stands for Test, Operate, Test, Exit.

The first test is the trigger for the strategy. In other words, how does the model know when to begin any particular process. The next part is the O or operation. This is how the model goes about doing what they do. Next is the second T or test. This is the part of the strategy that lets the model know when to stop. If the criteria for completion are reached then the E occurs which is Exit. If not, then the model will continue to run through the operation until they achieve completion.

Let us take the example of booking a new client. Our strategy for doing this is:

Test/Trigger: The enquiry comes in either by phone, letter or email

Operate: We endeavour to elicit all of the relevant information from the initial enquiry including if possible the fundamental reason for their seeking out therapy. Additionally, we attempt to ascertain the client's knowledge of therapy and which therapy will be appropriate. We then either book them or send them the relevant information by post or email. Even if the person books they receive a free brochure for reference.

Test: Have we sent out the relevant literature (the last step no matter whether the client booked for therapy or not) ?

Exit: If yes then exit; if no, return to the operation until the necessary information is gleaned so that the information pack can be sent.

Behaviour Integration

This is the final stage of modelling. Once you have all of the relevant information you need from the model relating to beliefs/values and strategies, you then observe the behaviour and determine what parts of the model's behaviour you would like to adapt for yourself. This component is often the hardest, because there is a chance that the person you have decided to model engages in a behaviour that ensures their success that you cannot or will not integrate into yourself. This is the reason why one can and should model as many different people as possible, so that if you find someone's behaviour is not in alignment with yours, you can still get something from the process, and get the necessary behavioural traits from a different model.

Modelling Exercise

Think of someone who is running a successful practice and do a modelling exercise with them.

From your observation, what do you imagine are their values and beliefs?

From your observation, what do you imagine are their strategies?

From your observation, what behaviours could you integrate into your own way of being?

When you have done this see how it feels and whether you need to make adjustments or whether it fits perfectly.

Blocks to success

After all that good positive stuff, here comes the bad news. But the good news is that the bad news can be turned around, and used to help you to be better and better. So let's not get too down.

We all have blocks to success. Yes, everyone, even the most successful people in the world have, or have had blocks. Blocks can vary, in size, strength and location.

For one person, a fear of rejection may block them from going out to get a job at all, whereas for another it may just block them from going for a key job. Another's belief that money is a "bad thing" may stop them from exploiting a share option that could earn them millions, for someone else it may mean that they refrain from charging an appropriate amount for their services. A childhood injunction to "be good" may dampen the competitive edge so that someone fails to promote their practice adequately, or an injunction of "don't feel" may stop another from risking forming the relationships required.

We feel a need to restate the fact that everyone has blocks. For example, a millionaire may have a block about getting to two million or an athlete may have a block about breaking a particular time barrier. Incidentally there are many sporting examples of barriers (such as the four minute mile) which, once broken by one person, are soon broken by many.

Blocks may be due to:

- Fear (I am afraid to..... in case.....)
- Beliefs (I do not believe that I can....)
- Values (It wouldn't be right to.....)
- Lack of confidence (I'm not good enough to....)
- Lack of thought (It never occurred to me that I could.....)

The techniques described in the section on Obstacles can be used here. It can be helpful to see a block as an obstacle that can be REMOVED, gone OVER, UNDER, AROUND or THROUGH, SHRUNK, or UTILISED. This reminds us of a conference presentation from Sharon and Jamie Lyn Thornton which likened psychological blocks to wooden blocks in karate. The crucial part of their presentation was that in order for a karate expert to break through a block of wood they need to think through and beyond the block; in this instance two feet beyond the block.

To use this metaphor in overcoming psychological blocks to success is obvious. Think through and beyond. For example, if you set yourself a goal of making £20,000 in a year, you are unlikely to make more, but if you set yourself a much higher goal, and envisage yourself achieving it, you may.

Sometimes we construct huge barriers....

My Blocks to Success

Without thinking, answer the following questions:

1. How much money would you like to make next year?

2. Will you do so?

3. (If you answered yes, go to Q8) Why not?

4. Are you afraid to? Do you feel any fear right now?

5. Does it contradict your beliefs or values?

6. Do you deserve it?

7. How are you going to get through this block?

8. Why did you choose that figure? Why not double it?

9. Would doubling your figure be scary or contradict your values or beliefs?

Revisit the idea of blocks regularly: once you clear one you will find another, and another, but you will get better at seeing them for what they are, and, importantly at clearing them.

Utilising your full potential

By this stage in the book you will have discovered much about yourself, and (we hope) made some changes and taken action to move forward in your career. There are lots of positive steps to take to help yourself to be a successful therapist, and by now you will know what many of these are.

It is now time to draw some of these threads together by looking at your potential. The authors have a very simple motto which we would like to share with you:

If other people can, I can.

There are limitations to this, of course. Neither of the authors could run 100m in 10 seconds however hard we tried (not a pretty picture), but we strongly believe that for the most part this is true. This rule can be applied to work and to other situations (you should see Fiona's hand built cupboards!), but we will concentrate here on this idea in terms of building your practice.

Are there successful people in your therapy in the UK? Unless you are practising something very obscure the answer will be yes. There are plenty of therapists of every ilk who make a full time living from their therapy work. However, sometimes it is difficult to tell who is really successful, and (as previously discussed) perceptions of success vary. The authors regularly hear therapists who exaggerate their success. For example saying they see 30 clients a week at £50 per session but who are not VAT registered. (Maybe they are earning that but defrauding Her Majesty).

So narrow down the previous question to your definition. Are there people earning the amount you would like to make? Are there people seeing the number of clients you would like to make? Are there people with enough spare income to go to the places or drive the car you would like?

If there are, then you can, if you maximise all the elements of a therapy practice.

Left brain / Right brain

We often hear about people having a dominant brain hemisphere which will make them have a tendency to be better at either analytical or creative processing (to put it very simply). We also hear that people use only a fraction of the brain's physical potential.

So we have a question to ask:

Why not have a really strong right hemisphere and a really strong left?

If this idea interests you, then the key is exercise. Just as the body's fitness is improved through exercise, so is the mind's. There is recent research that suggests that as people age, the tendency to become forgetful is due to lack of brain exercise rather than an inevitable process.

Here are some fun, easy to fit in, brain exercises:

1. Ask "what if" questions- the sillier the better, eg What if I paid myself a tip for every time I am nice to a client? Train yourself to ask "what if" questions a lot. As I (Fiona) write this now, I could ask "What if I put a nonsense sentence in the book, and offered a prize to the first person to find it? Would that help sales?"

2. Use metaphors and analogies, eg my job is like a flooded river, it spills over into everything and that makes people angry, or writing this book is like therapy, it analyses problems and offers resolution while being fun.

3. Daydream, eg fantasise about being the best therapist in your area and how everyone thinks you are wonderful

4. Pay attention to small ideas: from little acorns, great big oak trees grow

5. Use the Reverse Method, eg ask yourself, "how can I make less money?"

6. Use questioning to ask why and how as often as you can. Ask yourself and others. Most people love being asked questions about themselves. It shows you are interested and hence they are important. But please make sure you listen to the answers. One of the authors recently had the experience of talking to someone who asked lots of questions, maintained excellent eye contact and was skilled at appearing really interested, until he forgot to listen. Your interest in your clients needs to be genuine. As an aside, you may have noticed the trend for people to say that "politicians don't listen". There seems to be a presumption that listening means agreeing. You can listen to another person's argument, understand it, but still disagree.

Be interested in your clients

7. Play "just suppose", eg just suppose I got up half an hour earlier... or just suppose I did believe that I could do it...

8. Use drawing etc, eg draw your role as a therapist and then explain your drawing to your supervisor, or draw a tree and explain why it is like you

9. Use the non-dominant hand occasionally

10. Ask your unconscious to solve a problem or answer a question for you overnight

11. Write poems about your life and goals

12. Use handwriting sometimes (with a nice pen and use colours) rather than the computer

13. Do sums, eg balance your cheque book without using a calculator or add up the value of your shopping as you go around the supermarket.

14. When you are part way through a novel or video, stop and think up your own ending

15. Do jigsaws and crosswords: the harder the better! Other puzzles too, such as logic puzzles or tsunami.

16. Set yourself a task of learning something new to expand the hemisphere of your brain that you perceive to be weaker. For example if you are a naturally creative person read a book on nuclear physics and if you are more analytical have a go at painting.

Providing the best service you can

In writing this book we have presumed that you are qualified and competent in your chosen therapy. However we are aware that there are too many people in the world of complementary therapies who go into practice without proper training. This will vary from therapy to therapy, especially as regulation varies from strict control to no control at all.

We believe that in order to provide an ethical service, you must know what you are doing. You need to become an expert in your field, if you are not already. Not only is this vital for your clients' well being, it is vital for your success too.

Later in this book there is a section on continuing professional development, but this does not take the place of a good grounding in your therapy. Most therapies have benchmark qualifications which you can check by asking the professional societies. In some therapies there are various opinions on requirements so check thoroughly and please ensure that you get yourself up to the necessary standard before working with clients.

This book cannot be specific in maximising your skills and knowledge. However, there is a plan on the following page that you can use to ensure that you consistently work on this key area.

Skills and Knowledge Plan

Periodically use this sheet to analyse where you are and where you need to go in terms of skills and knowledge.

There is always something to learn, something to improve: this is a good thing: it means you can grow.

Area to be worked on	How?	When?

What do you offer?

Do you know exactly what you are offering? Can you define what you do, why you do it and the benefits that your clients can expect? You probably have answered yes, but we would encourage you to think this through thoroughly with the exercises that follow.

In many therapies there are two distinct modalities of therapy, namely prevention and "cure". We have put cure in quotation marks as it is often unethical to use this word when relating to clients. However, in this context we are looking at those problems which you and your client are attempting to resolve. If your therapy has these modalities, you may like to do the exercises for the modalities separately and have distinct areas in your marketing materials or even separate marketing plans. For example, an osteopath may offer preventative care to sports people as a completely discrete service.

It is, of course, important that you know what you do, but it is even more so that you can impart this information to your potential clients. They need to know why they should come to you rather than anyone else from the same or a different therapy, and indeed rather than doing nothing.

- What will they gain by coming to you?
- What will they lose by not coming to you?

It can be very useful to look at these factors from different angles. Put yourself in the client's position to ascertain what they really need. Look at things from the position of someone older or younger than you, or someone from a different background, and from those of the opposite gender.

You can also look at how others describe their role, and learn from other therapies and professions as well as your own. Sometimes the realisation that you don't like someone else's method can be as illuminating as agreeing. For example, the authors attended a seminar on coaching at which the presenters displayed some attitudes that they believed were unethical and unprofessional (stating that clients bore them and promoting collusion among other things). This experience helped clarify the strong ethical ground that the authors have adopted in writing this book.

In specifying the three elements of a therapy practice it is critical to remember that in order to be successful you must be providing what the potential client wants and needs, not what you believe they ought to want and need. One of the authors recalls being on holiday in Bali, where this concept was clearly demonstrated by high-pressure sales tactics from taxi drivers. We didn't want to go anywhere, but still they would pester and offer cheaper rates and claim superiority over their rivals. We expect that all our readers have experienced the cold-calling double-glazing salesman who also does not seem to realise that if you don't want windows, you don't want windows.

The product you offer must be what the client needs

What You Offer Exercise

State as clearly as you can what you are offering:

What needs, desires or opportunities of your client does this address?

What are the tangible benefits to your client?

What are the intangible benefits?

What are the short and long -term benefits?

Service Exercise

Review the information on the pain/pleasure principle on p18 and then write down below 20 negative or painful things that potential clients may experience if they don't have your therapy and 20 positive or pleasurable things they may experience if they do.

Pain	Pleasure

Dealing with negativity

We have discussed your own process at length in "Being the best therapist you can be", but we have included negativity in this section, as much of this has to do with the service that you provide. You may encounter negativity in the following ways:

- Doubt in your therapy from:
  - Potential clients
  - Family and friends
  - The medical profession
- Doubt in your ability from:
  - Yourself
  - Family and friends
  - Competitors
- Doubt in your ability to succeed from
  - Yourself
  - Family and friends
- Reaction to your efforts (eg dissatisfied clients)
- Mistakes

It isn't always sunny

The key to all these situations is preparation. If you think through all possible negative scenarios you can often prevent them from occurring by taking pre-emptive action. For example:

- Dispel clients' doubts by giving full and frank information in literature and in all discussions
- Get an in-depth knowledge of your subject so that you can refute criticisms from safe and strong ground
- Practice reframing (see p157)
- Set up procedures to use in cases of self-doubt
- Find people with whom you can talk through any negativity
- Remember that mistakes are inevitable but that preparation can minimise them and that mistakes can be seen as opportunities to learn. Also remember to learn from other people's mistakes.
- Bear in mind that you cannot help everyone and there is a category of client who will always complain (any experienced therapist will know the phenomenon).

You and your competition

It is unlikely that you are in an area with no competition, so who you are competing with, directly and indirectly will have a significant impact on your business. If you are applying for a loan to support your practice you will be expected to produce a detailed analysis of your competition.

Maybe it's advisable to avoid locking horns with your competition

You will need to:
- Investigate who are your direct and indirect competitors
- Check in what ways your services compete
- See if you can you fit in so that you complement each other
- Look into areas where you can specialise
- Check whether the market is big enough for all
- Work with your competition to support each other, if you can

*P*lanning Your Business

Writing a business plan

Many people think that you only need a business plan if you are going to apply for a loan. We disagree. If we think back to the section on goal setting, we looked at the fact that if you don't know where you are going you are unlikely to get there. The business plan is a formalised goal setting procedure.

Your plan should include the following sections:

1. Summary
2. The Business
3. Markets and competitors
4. Sales and marketing
5. Management
6. Operations
7. Financial forecasts
8. Financial requirements
9. Assessing risks

We will now look at these sections in more detail. For the sake of completeness, we will presume that you are wanting a bank loan to cover your first six months operating costs. (If you don't, then your plan will be simpler).

Summary

Even though this section goes first, it should be written last and should contain the crucial elements of the plan in a précised form. Bankers (like most people), don't want to read reams of information, so give them the basics and excite their interest to do business with you here.

The Business

In this section you need to explain your therapy, how you intend to run your business (hours of operation, location, facilities.) and any other elements of your practice such as product sales. Remember that your audience is likely to be unaware of things that you might take for granted. Check this section out with some friends who do not understand your therapy to see if it makes sense. On the other hand you are not training your banker to be a therapist so you do not have to write a book.

Markets and competitors

Who will be your clients? What sort of people, what sort of presenting issues, where are they? Who are your direct and indirect competitors (see p74)? On this you are likely to need to do some research. We will use the example of George who, having just qualified, is setting up a new acupuncture clinic. He needs to find out who else offers acupuncture in his area. This may include medical practitioners as well as those whose main therapy is acupuncture. He needs to find out who offers related therapies such as acupressure or other meridian therapies, and maybe (if he is intending to offer smoking cessation), hypnotherapists.

He also needs to find out how they charge, how and where they advertise and where they work.

Part of this section will be setting out your pricing policy. It can be difficult to set your charges, but we recommend that you follow these points:

- Charging too little can cause potential clients to perceive your value as lower than your competitors
- Charging too much can cause potential clients to choose a competitor who they feel offers better value for money
- Charges should be clear and simple
- If you charge VAT, state this clearly in all marketing materials as it will enhance your credibility

Give all these details in this section, being as thorough as you can be. The bank needs to know that you can make money.

Sales and marketing

In this section explain how you are going to market your practice and how you are going to advertise. Go into details about the sales you expect to generate from these processes and give grounds for your expectations.

Management

Here you give information about yourself, your qualifications and background to enable the banker to see that you have the abilities required to make a success of your business.

Operations

The bank also nccds to know the details of how you intend to run your business. For example where you will practice from, how you will furnish your premises, any staff requirements and legal implications.

Financial forecasts

Your financial forecasts need to show how and when you will be able to pay off your debt. Make them detailed and realistic. Show growth and allow for situations such as illness or holidays. If you put in that you will have 20 clients a week from the off, every week, 52 weeks of the year, the banker will be sceptical and lose confidence in the accuracy of the other information you provide.

Include graphs where possible.

Financial requirements

Explain exactly what you need and what it is for. Also show what it is not for, ie those items that you have already got covered. Demonstrate a clear, rational and realistic thought process.

Assessing risks

Again this is an opportunity for you to demonstrate your rational thinking and your openness and honesty. Brainstorm anything that can go wrong and outline your contingency plans. Consider what would happen if you or a member of your family became ill, if something happened to your premises, if competition suddenly increased, if the law changed regarding your therapy and also remember to consider things that are specific to your circumstances (and things we may have forgotten to mention!)

Ensure you know what risks you are taking

Premises

One of the most important choices that any therapist has to make is from where to practise. Opinions differ over the professionalism of working from home, but the obvious advantage is cost. Below we will list the possibilities highlighting the pros and cons of each option.

Home

Pros:

- You do not have to pay for premises
- You may be able to claim tax relief for a proportion of your utility bills (please consult with your accountant for exact details)
- Convenience. No transport, parking etc to consider
- You avoid having unproductive gaps in your schedule
- You are in charge of the environment
- Some clients feel more comfortable in a home setting

Cons:

- Some clients feel that you are less professional in this setting
- Setting up your home to be suitable can be difficult. Some therapies have laws stipulating requirements such as have a wash basin in the room. If in doubt check the requirements for your therapy with your professional society.
- Your family may be inconvenienced
- Your sessions may be disturbed by your family
- It may be harder for you to "switch off" out of hours
- Isolation from other therapists
- Where will clients wait? If you allow waiting, you are allowing people to enter your home unaccompanied and thus exposing yourself to risk.
- Will you be safe?
- Possibility of capital gains tax and business rates. Consult your accountant.

If you decide to take this option then we suggest that you:

- Make the approach to the house as tidy as possible: mow the lawn, put toys away, paint the front door...
- Make your consulting room seem as professional as possible.
- (If you are using the lounge), remove clutter and install a desk.
- Do not use a room with a bed in it.
- Set up work and non-work rituals so that you can switch off
- Ensure adequate access to a loo
- Minimise contact with other parts of the house: your clients do not want to see your kitchen full of dirty washing
- Train your family
- Keep pets well away
- Dress formally and act as you would if you were operating from an office
- Set up a system for waiting. If you do not have facilities for a waiting area, inform clients when booking that they should not be early and stick to your session times rigidly
- Ensure client records are held securely
- Check your home insurance policies to ensure you are covered for this. See resources section for details.
- Consider measures to ensure your safety
- Consult your accountant to ensure you do not have to pay capital gains tax and business rates.

Renting consulting rooms

There are various ways to do this. You can rent by the hour / session /day / week in

- GP surgeries
- Complementary health centres
- Health food shops
- Beauty or hairdressing salons
- Sports centres

Pros:

- Good marketing opportunities
- Chances to network with other therapists
- Helps the professional image
- May have reception facilities
- Gives you clear working boundaries

Cons:

- Cost. Charges vary greatly, but you may find that you are paying for time that you do not use.
- You are not in control of the environment and facilities
- Some potential clients may be concerned about being seen going to a "clinic"

Your own premises

Pros:

- You control the environment
- Professional image
- You may be able to rent space to other therapists
- Gives you clear working boundaries

Cons:

- Cost

Mobile therapy

By this we mean providing home visits. However, the authors know of a hypnotherapists in the USA who travels around in a huge camper van equipped as a consulting room, which could work here, but probably not in central London.

Pros:

- There is no cost for the facility
- This may expand your client base as some potential clients would prefer a home visit and for some it is a necessity

Cons:

- You have no control over the environment
- Your client is more likely to be distracted by everyday events, people and other elements of their home environment.
- You will have no external ways of demonstrating your professionalism, just you.
- Travel time and cost
- You will need to bring everything with you, which may not be a problem for a counsellor, but would be harder for an aromatherapist.
- Safety

Conclusion

You may well already have a clear idea of the better alternative for you, or you may decide to try out a couple of options. There is no reason why you shouldn't practice from several places to start with as you build up your practice.

Both the authors have worked from different bases, but both now run their private practices exclusively from home. They have chosen to have homes where they can have a room set up on the ground floor, that while used for other purposes (important for capital gains tax reasons), looks and feels like an office, while being comfortable and inviting.

Neither author has waiting facilities. All clients are informed of this and neither author has had a problem in this regard in their combined 23 years of practice.

Financial considerations

We will not go into details here, except to say the following must be considered, and revisited on a regular basis:

- Premises costs
- Utility costs
- Phone costs
- Marketing costs
- Accountancy costs (do not avoid this: you need their advise)
- Possibility of capital gains tax
- Possibility of business rates
- Insurance (practice / contents / buildings)
- National Insurance
- Income tax
- VAT

*A*ccessing your market

Marketing

In order to survive as a practitioner of any discipline, the general public as well as other interested parties need to know you exist. This getting your name out is called marketing.

When marketing your practice there are several things that you will need to consider:

*W*hat is the need for Marketing?

Simply put, if you do not market yourself, you will not get clients, if you do not get clients you will not survive in practice. It really is as simple as that. Marketing is the way we get our names about. Let us illustrate by the example of when one of the authors (Shaun) bumped into an ex-student and asked him "How's business?" He replied that though he had been qualified for 8 months, he had not yet seen a client. Shaun was shocked so pressed him further and he revealed that he had done no marketing or advertising; he assumed that simply because he was a qualified therapist people would come.

Although this is an extreme example, it is a commonly held belief that since GP's do not need to market themselves neither do therapists. This is clearly not the case. Even now GP's are engaged in marketing themselves more than they have at any time since the establishment of the National Health Service.

In this section we will explain what marketing strategies have worked for us and colleagues of ours and how you can make them work for you as well.

Marketing includes:

Marketing includes all things that come into contact with the public that are related to you. This is not advertising per se (advertising is covered in detail later in this book). Marketing includes the materials you use, the places you promote yourself, and how you promote yourself as well as how you communicate with the public. We use the term public here to denote "everyone". There are likely specifics in marketing for different groups within that classification, perhaps members of your own therapeutic community or the allopathic medical community.

Presentation is one of the most important things for the development of a successful and ethical practice. Having said that, it is important to remember the elements of a therapy practice. In other words, practitioners who do presentation well but have no substance will not survive long term.

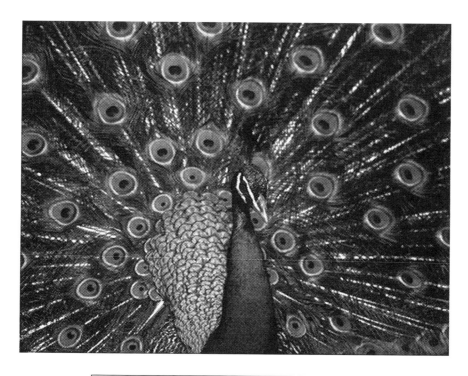

Let the world know you are there!

Below are listed some of the aspects which we consider to be important components of marketing

Telephone Answering: Personal

This is perhaps where most mistakes can be made regarding your interface with the public. Remember, first impressions are the most important. When answering the phone there are several points to consider. The most important is to sound professional. When clients ring my (Shaun's) office they hear "Brookhouse Hypnotherapy how may I help you?" It is short and to the point, yet also professional. I have rung numerous therapists over the years, and have had my calls answered from anything ranging from "What?" to "Yes" to "Mummy is not here" to "0161 XXXXXXXX". These answers are all flawed for obvious, and some not quite so obvious reasons.

Short one or two word salutations are inappropriate because one does not know that one has rung the right number without some form of identification. The caller needs to hear more than a couple of syllables in order to be able to process the information correctly. In addition, clients can be nervous, indeed too nervous to be sure that they have rung the correct number.

Short answers to calls also give the impression that the person answering has better things to do than to speak to you. This may well be true: a good rule of thumb is to not answer the phone unless you have time to talk. If you do not, leave it to the answering machine to deal with.

The "Mummy is not here" answer is common in home based offices. If you work from home, we advise a separate line for your practice and/or ensuring that your phone is answered only by yourself or your machine. Nothing sounds more unprofessional than having a child answer your phone. We have also heard examples of partners, flatmates or parents answering the phone and saying inappropriate things. For example: "Darling, it's for you...", "He's at work at the moment" or "Tell me what you want help with and I'll stick a note on his door".

A good professional telephone manner needs to be developed. You may need to work on how to sound confident without being pushy. You may be desperate to get the potential client to book, but as an ethical practitioner you need to remember that it is only right for them to book with you if it IS right for them to book with you. Also, sounding desperate does not sound professional.

Remember as well, when you are answering calls you are not only giving information you are receiving information as well. You will be eliciting the caller's name, address, and phone number as well as presenting issues and convenient times for appointments.

Finally, answering the phone with a number has many of the same disadvantages to answering with a one or two word phrase. Often times the number is given too quickly and the client is left with the same confusion as earlier pointed out. It also does not sound professional. How many businesses do you know of that say a number rather than a name?

Telephone Answering: Machine

No therapist is able to answer all their calls personally, simply because they cannot answer the phone when they are with a client. If you currently break into a client's session to answer the phone, please reconsider. The client is paying for your time and attention, which should be given to them 100%, barring emergencies.

Therefore you need to consider your answerphone message very carefully to minimise hang-ups and maximise your business. In many cases people who are looking for a therapist will pick up a Yellow Pages and go through the list until someone answers the phone. This problem can be minimised with either a receptionist, an answering service, or a really good voice mail message.

The advantages of having a receptionist are obvious, but if your practice is so successful that you can hire one, you probably wouldn't be reading this book. However, it may be that you use premises with an "inbuilt" receptionist, in which case the comments about answering services below will apply.

Answering services have a certain appeal to them in that the potential client is going to end up speaking to a real person rather than a machine. A disadvantage to the answering service is that you cannot control what is being said in your name and how it is being said. One cannot, with the best will in the world, make a minimum wage telephonist sound particularly enthusiastic about your service.

With answering machines, you are far more in control of what is being said and when you will be able to get back to the potential client. A common mistake we have found listening to practitioners' answering machines is that practitioners often state that they are out. A potential client might well wonder why you are out of the office during ordinary working hours. This is especially relevant for part time practitioners who are out at their "day job" from 9-5. Clients by and large want what they view as a full time professional practitioner, not someone who "does it on the side".

The message Shaun uses for his practice is:

"Hello and thank you for calling Brookhouse Hypnotherapy, my name is Shaun Brookhouse. If you are calling between 9am and 9pm, I am probably with a client and am unable to take your call at the moment. If you would like to book an appointment, please leave your name, telephone number and a convenient time to call, and I will return your call. If you would like a free brochure, please leave your name address and telephone number, spelling any unusual words and one will be posted to you as soon as possible. All of the details of this practice can be found on the Internet at www.hypno-nlp.com Thank you again for calling.

To the casual observer, this might seem a particularly long message (it is 58 seconds long), but it does many things.

- It shows clients that I am not speaking to them because I am working with someone else. Clients, paradoxically want two things from the therapist, one to be busy and two to be exclusive to them. In other words clients want to believe that you work only for them, but also want you to be busy. This message is on all the time, even if I am teaching on the weekend, it is meant to imply a very busy practice. In our case this is true, but for a part-timer, this could be a way for you to be able to not return calls for several hours whilst you are working elsewhere and still get people to leave messages.
- It gives my hours of operation of 9 until 9. This is often one of the first questions asked by clients, "Do you do evenings?" Well, the answering machine has just answered that for me. The message gives the potential client the ability to determine when the call back should be or whether they would prefer to have a free brochure first.
- It gives our website, which shows that the practice is a large professional concern and that they can find the information they need direct from there before coming for an appointment.
- It sounds professional but still personal. The question asking for a convenient time to call shows caring, and the promise to send the brochure as soon as possible shows commitment. Please note that any promises such as this must be fulfilled.

Your Telephone Number

Although there is not much choice with telephone numbers, there is some. You may opt to have a free phone number (typically 0800), which may bring a slight advantage in that potential clients do not have to pay to enquire. However, this is balanced by the fact that this costs you considerably more, and also, if a person will quibble about paying for a phone call, are they likely to be happy to pay for therapy?

There is one place, however, where an 0800 number will definitely help and that is for people who are wanting to place a call from their workplace, but would not be allowed to make a charged call.

Many therapists give their mobile number as their contact number for potential clients. This has benefits in that you can be accessed wherever you are (except on the tube, up a mountain, on a plane....) but some clients still have the belief that ringing a mobile is expensive, so think carefully about your intended market. If you are aiming at 18-25 year old professionals, then a mobile number is fine. If you market is predominantly over 45 then you may reconsider.

Depending on your age, you may remember when phone numbers were given as letters. All old dialling phones had letters by the numbers. This went out of fashion, but with texting it is returning, particularly in the USA. The trend is sure to follow here. It may be that you can get a number that in letters will refer to you. (Eg 07xxx x49766 could be written out as 07xxx xHYPNO).

You may also, of course, try to get a number that is easily memorable. Listen to some of the numbers given out on radio stations and you will see some options.

Business Cards

Business cards are so often neglected by practitioners as being an irrelevance or luxury which they do not need. There is a cultural element to the use of business cards. Go to the USA and you will find everyone uses them all the time. If you do not have cards for clients or potential clients to take away with them, it is likely that they will not contact you when the need for your services arises. Many people are not good with names so when they are asked "Who was that homoeopath you went to see?" The reply is often, "I can't remember her name, I am sure you can find one in Yellow Pages". The problem here is clear, you did all the work in cultivating this prospect, even so far as to treat them therapeutically, and another therapist, who you cannot guarantee will be as good as you is going to benefit because you did not give her a card.

We suggest that you do not scrimp on cards. Have them professionally produced, preferably in colour but tasteful. A good quality card may be in circulation for years so you want it professionally produced so that the ink does not run and/or it gets crushed and thrown out because it is too flimsy. If your card is professional and classy, the client is more likely to hold on to it as being something of value. At an unconscious level they will see a black and white version on thin card as being more "disposable", and by inference, your practice as being less professional. Cards produced on a computer never look good enough (in our humble opinion: let us have an example if you disagree!)

Use fonts which are easily readable, (times, ariel, etc.) Avoid fancy scripts like this or this or this . Pleasing to the eye as they may be, a card must be easily read. Finally, NEVER use old English fonts as your text. Many years ago, Shaun had a card produced in old English because he thought it would be classy; he threw the lot away without using one because when they came back from the printers he could not read them, each one just looked like a great blob of ink on the card.

Other business card tips:

- Shop around for printers. Costs vary hugely. See p109
- Use your logo (if you have one: see p108)
- Consider the card content very carefully. It needs to say enough but not be cluttered. It is important that the recipient, on finding the card two years later, has enough information to know who you are and what you do.
- Ensure that the recipient will be able to contact you from the card. Phone numbers and addresses can change, so we suggest you put both landline and mobile numbers, and an email address so that wherever you end up, the chances are that one will remain.
- Always put your website address on the card so that the recipient can find out more about you easily.
- See p108 for a discussion on the use of photos in marketing materials.

Stationery

With stationery you have a choice as to whether to produce your own on a computer or have it printed by a professional printer. If you print your own the rules are the same as for business cards. Clarity in typeface and quality of paper are important. We would recommend the judicious use of colour as well; some colour gives a professional appearance, but a lot can appear tacky.

Some tips for stationery:

- If you choose to have your stationery professionally produced, shop around for printers. Costs vary hugely. See p109
- Use your logo (if you have one: see p108)
- Ensure that all your stationery matches: your letterheads, compliments slips, flyers, brochures and cards should all follow the same theme. Envelopes should also blend in (and be neatly addressed).
- Consider the content very carefully. Letterheads and compliments slips need to say enough but not be cluttered. It is important that the recipient has enough information to be able to respond easily. We have seen many badly designed letterheads, for example, not including a phone number, or without a printed name with an illegible signature.
- Always put your website address on all stationery so that the recipient can find out more about you easily.
- See p109 for a discussion on the use of photos in marketing materials.

Brochures

The authors strongly believe in giving brochures to all potential clients; even those who book a session straight without receiving one beforehand receive one at their first session. A brochure can be used in a similar way to the business card, and again it is important to maximise the quality so that recipients feel it is something worth holding on to.

Ensure your brochures give all the information that potential clients will need in order to make the decision to see you:

- Name (yes, we know it's obvious, but we've seen brochures which just give the business name)
- Full contact details including website, email and phone number(s)
- Location(s)
- Practice hours
- Details of your qualifications, training, memberships and experience
- Types of therapy offered and their benefits
- Prices and cancellation policy
- Frequently asked questions
- Possibly a list of issues that you work with, but see p113 for a discussion on this

Below we detail some ideas, partly developed by Gill Drury. We reproduce her ideas with her kind permission.

There are many books available on design and we have seen many different examples of both effective and non-effective marketing materials. Indeed we have experimented with many different styles and approaches ourselves. Defining good design is largely a matter of opinion. What is good to one person, or to one company, may not be good to another. It depends on you, your therapy, your specific objective and your target audience.

For our purposes let's define good design to mean:

"Good design is effective at gaining the readers attention and getting the results you want ."

If you plan to do it yourself, remember the acronym **AIDA**.

Attract   **A**TTENTION

Arouse   **I**NTEREST

Create   **D**ESIRE

Stimulate   **A**CTION

Headlines & Titles
- You have 1.7 seconds to gain someone's attention
- 55% of readers are pulled in by a banner headline
- Get their attention with an action word or verb
- Evoke an image or mood, paint a picture
- Provide some kind of information

 Photographs (see p108)
- 28% are pulled in by a photography
- Use action photos – eyes focused on something
- Smile!
- Captions are there to answer the question – why is the photo/picture there?
- As a rule captions tend to be read before body copy – however long
- Put a piece of information in the caption that will be missed if someone doesn't read the body copy

 Choose Short or Long Body Text
- Short sections of copy (50 words or less) can be used to divide up your brochure
- Use side bars – very useful to create short sections
- Précis the information – give tips
- The eye then goes to sub-headings – so break up the copy
- Today we are in a visual society – not one that reads a lot – You have to get the scanners visually
- Long Body text gives much more flexibility to use graphic devices

 Non-photographic Art
- Buy in clip art – available on CD packages
- If someone you know can draw – use them
- You can also use cartoons, illustrations, icons, graphs, charts, diagrams
- If you have 5 or more numbers in your text it's wise to add a chart/diagram

Numbers/Outlines

- Keep specific and memorable
- Use numbers in headlines
- Make numerals dramatic
- Choose unusual numbers –not divisible by 5 or 10
- Use big numbers for big offers
- If 8 pages in length or more use a table of contents
- If 4-8 pages long use a 'what's inside box'

Graphic Devices

- Use "exclamation marks" with restraint
- A graphic device is a symbol that means something to those who share a common language
- Keylines are also a graphic device
- Pick two or three per publication. Use them consistently throughout the publication.
- You could use large initial letters to indicate the beginning of a chapter, increased to 3/5 times the size of the body text.
- Use graphics that are relevant to the text.
- Use your company logo as a graphic element (see p108). Consider incorporating it into your brochures nameplate, as a stop device, or as part of a border in a brochure.

Readability and Screens

- Black is the only colour that works well on itself
- Use a screen no darker that 30% with black text
- Light/white text use no lighter than 70%

0%	10%	30%	50%	60%	70%	90%	100%
Compare	the	contrast	as	screen	density	increases	
	the	contrast	as	screen	density	increases	and decreases
	the	contrast	as	screen	density	increases	and decreases

Boxes and Bullet Points

Boxes tell the reader 'this is a primary point'. Bullet points relate to one another. Use boxes and bullets the same way you would use a traditional outline.

■ Boxes catch the eye, and readers expect a summary point. If it interests them they will read on
 	
   • Boxes facilitate scanning
   • They enable the reader to pick out key words or concepts
   • A series of box points prepares your readers for the correct quantity of information and thus they will feel neither overwhelmed or disappointed
	1. Using a traditional outline signals a certain formality
	
	   1.1. It is a conventional format, familiar to most readers
	   1.2. It is tried and tested; it works well as a tool to organise data, concepts, facts or theories

■ Bullet points serve multiple purposes.
Readers expect each bullet point within a grouping to be related
 	
   • Because bullet points are indented, copy appears easier to read than if it were set as regular narrative text
   • Bullet points appear livelier than other outline formats, an image you may wish to convey
	If you want to appear academic, an outline is a good choice ·
	
	   A If you use the outline format, you should adhere to the conventions
	   B For lively, fun, or exciting messages, avoid using an outline

Tips for writing
- Be reader oriented - use 'you'
- WIIFM – what's in it for me
- Write conversationally but grammatically correctly
- Read it out loud
- Stress the benefits
- Write at a "low" level. Educated people will not be offended, and all will understand. Not too low though.

Proof
- Offer proof in the form of research findings
- Statistics: but only if you have the properly conducted research to back them up
- Simple benefits

Call to Action
- Tell the potential client exactly what to do next
- Tell them how to do it
- Tell them when to do it
- Tell them what they can expect to happen

Layout design

Balance

Symmetrical
In symmetrically balanced layouts, copy is centred and art is distributed evenly. A symmetrical presentation is likely to be perceived as conventional, conservative, traditional, academic, formal, stable.

Asymmetrical
In asymmetrical layouts, use unusual shapes, white space and colour to achieve balance. An asymmetrical layout is likely to be perceived as visually exciting, surprising, abstract, jazzy, interesting, creative, informal, modern, friendly.

An example of a symmetrical layout:

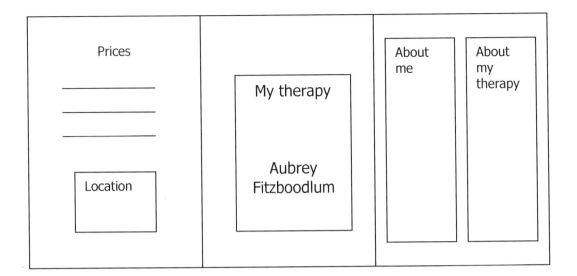

An example of an asymmetrical layout:

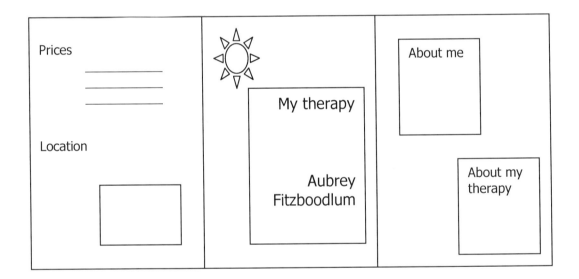

To achieve balance use optical weight

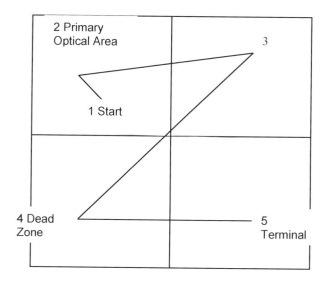

There are six rules of balance

1 Anything located in the upper left quadrant (the primary optical area) of a layout is more heavily weighted than anything located anywhere else.

2 Large items are noticed more, seen for a longer time, and remembered better than are small items.

3 Elements that are dark carry more optical weight than elements that are light

4 Colour conveys more optical weight than black and white – use with restraint

5 White space serves to draw the reader's attention to whatever is in the 'non empty' space, Counterbalance v important.

6 Rectangles are usual shapes. Everything else conveys optical weight. This means squares, triangles, ovals, circles, elliptical shapes, cubes and others all convey optical weight. Unusual shapes are more interesting.

Colour

The placement of colour on the right creates a powerful symmetry.

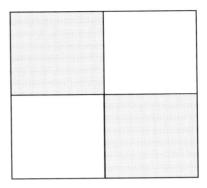

Rules/Borders

Rules and Borders are effective devices if you want to encourage the reader to perceive a two page spread as one unit. See below.

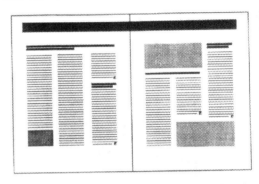

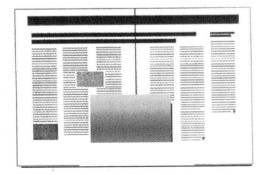
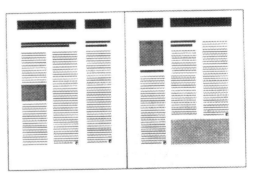

Unity

Achieve unity by using graphic devices and elements of unity consistently. Only change these if you change your objectives, audience or message and only change 2 or 3 at a time.

Seven design options contribute to unity:

1   **Typography** – 2 fonts per publication (headlines, sub-headings, body text)
2   **Paper** – Stock – marry paper to the theme/industry
3   **Style of art** – only use one style per publication
4   **Colour** – colour is powerful – don't go too pastel
    Colour means different things – in the UK blue is the favourite colour, South Africa – green + yellow, North America – burgundy
    Warm colours have a yellow undertone
    Red or orange – people are automatically pulled to you
    Green – reassuring
    Metallic – quality and elegance
5   **Size** – Use size wisely to balance your work
6   **Graphic elements** – Use 2 to 3 consistently
7   **Grid** – Proportion of the piece

Proportion

Proportion refers to the underlying skeleton of your layout. Take advantage of desktop publishing's flexibility.

One Column Grid: Use when you want the reader to perceive your layouts as newsy or important, or when you have one element you want to stand out, such as a headline, photograph or logo.

Two Column Grid: Use to create a formal, conservative look. Perceived by readers as technical, scientific, conservative, regulatory, complex, academic, and traditional. Put a tilt in to make it less formal.

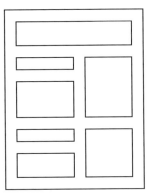

Three Column Grid: These layouts allow for more flexibility than the other two. They are livelier and tend to be viewed by readers as informal, relaxed, friendly, very easy to read.

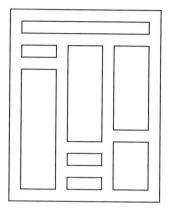

Tri Folds or Third A4

A third A4 leaflet is a handy size. It is inexpensive to produce, fits easily into envelopes and provides plenty of room for copy.

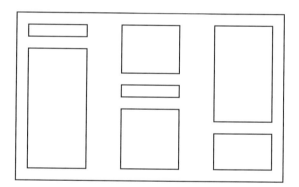

No matter what size layout you are creating ensure

- You allow adequate white space.

- You make the pages look interesting.

- You include graphics, artwork, shorter articles.

Clarity and Emphasis

- Make sure your first, second and third most important things are seen with ease
- Have a purposeful design: ask yourself:
    1. What is your objective?
    2. Who are your readers? Visualise them and jot down some key words.
    3. What is the most important element?
    4. What do you want them to see first, second, third?
    5. What actions do you hope they will take?

Column Justification

Ragged Right Text	Justified Text
Increases comprehension by 55% Most readable Casual, informal	More formal Need good desktop publishing Creates hyphens and white space *Problems* Rivers of white space lead to vertical pull Narrow columns create uneven word spacing
Centred Text	**Ragged Left Text**
Reader will see shapes It demands more effort from your reader *Problems* It is difficult to find the beginning of each line	Only works if a strong graphic on the left or not much text Difficult to read – creates anxiety *Problems* It demands much more effort from your reader

Type Image

Serif – Serif types are highly readable. Its hooks, feet and brackets, and the differential between thick and thin parts contribute to its legibility, and in general the more legible a typeface, the more readable it is.

Bookman - Extremely legible often used in books

Garamond - Very elegant, good for body copy

Palatino - Almost calligraphy

Times Roman - Most commonly used worldwide, emphasises content not font

Sans Serif – Sans Serif type is perceived as modern, cosmopolitan, scientific and up to date. While people read sans serif type faster, they also tend to read it less accurately.

Lucida - Modern, cosmopolitan, sophisticated

Eras - Scientific quality

Berlin - Clean, not terrific body copy

Arial – Has almost become the standard font for those bored with Times

Comic Sans – a lighter, softer font while still readable

Logos

- A logo can add identity to your therapy practice
- A well designed logo will subliminally convey YOU to your potential clients
- If you are not a skilled designer have a logo professionally designed.
- Commercial printers can draft logos. However beware of committing yourself to costs without knowing whether you will like the results. Ask to see samples before you commission a designer.
- There are companies (search on the Internet) who specialise in logo design.
- If you choose to have one, ensure the colours and style fit with the image you wish to portray.

Use of Photos

- Only use your photo in your publicity materials if it will assist you in attracting clients. And not just clients, but the right sort of clients! We thought long and hard before including this point as we would not wish to offend anyone, but we have decided it is too important to be TOO concerned with your sensibilities.
- Use a professionally produced photo and dress professionally for the photo. Glamour shots may make you look a million dollars, but may not project the right image. Equally a picture of you gardening may show you as an approachable human being but again may not attract the clients you want.
- Look approachable in your photo. Not too serious and not like a rabbit caught in the headlights. But not laughing hysterically either!
- Look through the section on appearance (p54) before having your photo taken
- Use other photos sparingly, and only if they are relevant.

Printing

- Get at least three quotes for every print job - you will be amazed at the range of cost estimates. Here is the information you should provide the printer with when requesting a quote.

1   Brief description of the job
2   Quantity
3   Paper
4   Ink colour
5   Bleeds
6   Trim size
7   Folding, stapling, collating or other special services
8   Delivery arrangements
9   Photos or artwork
10   Pre- print proofs

- It may be worth asking the printers for copies of their estimating forms so you can use them to give the printer the information they require in the format they use so ensuring accurate quotes
- Most large commercial printers run predictable colours on predictable days of the week. If your job can wait until the appropriate colour day and if you can use standard colours you will save the cost of an additional colour.

Leaflets

Leaflets tend to be A5, printed on one or two sides, and are designed to promote interest and generate action. The design rules given for brochures apply to leaflets too, but particular attention needs to be given to the immediacy of your message.

Leaflets may be delivered door to door, inserted into newspapers or handed out on street corners. They may also be provided at venues such as surgeries, sports centres, health food shops or the local newsagent.

There are several things to remember when considering leafleting:

- Design your leaflet appropriately for your market. For example, if you are doing a leaflet drop in an up-market part of town, use high quality materials.
- Most of your leaflets will go straight in the bin. A one percent response rate on leaflet distribution would be high. A quarter of one percent response is a more realistic target.
- Including a voucher on your leaflet will add to its perceived value and so its retention rate will be higher
- Most people who get to the point of glancing at your leaflet will not, at that time, feel they need your service. Maybe they do, but if not, they may know someone who does. Can you design your leaflet to make a connection to that possible need?
- Ensure that your leaflet fits with the image that you are trying to promote.

Advertising

Yellow Pages is often the life blood of advertising in a therapy practice. Despite all of the major developments on how to market a practice, the most successful means of advertising for the majority of practitioners consulted is and always has been Yellow Pages. However, this is not an absolute, so we suggest you consult other therapists with your specialism in your area, or other areas with a similar profile.

Yellow Pages now also has a major Internet presence www.yell.com There is also the Talking Pages which has not proved beneficial for the authors but may be for others. If you have had success with this please let us know.

All advertising will depend on how much you are prepared to invest; Yellow Pages can be very effective, but only as effective as you are prepared to be. There are do's and don'ts to this in the same way there are for all other types of advertising. First you must consider how much are you prepared to spend. This is a personal choice based on a number of different factors. How many clients will you need to see to re-coop the costs of the advertising? What size of advertisement? What do you put into the ad? These questions will be addressed now.

How Many Clients Will You Need to See to Re-coop Your Investment?

This is a very important concern before making your decision as to the investment you want to make. One of the authors (Shaun) spends just under £2500 with Yell every year. This includes the Yellow Pages, Yell.Com (3 Entries with weblink Hypnotherapy, Psychotherapy, and Counselling) and their new Directory Enquiry Service. In his record keeping each week at the bottom of the diary there is Y/P with two figures after it. The first is the total income generated by Yell Products that week, and the second number is the running total of monies earned. The 2002-2003 Yellow Pages for Manchester came out in mid August; by the first week of November, he had re-cooped his entire investment for the year, which of course means, that everything else earned on Yell Products this year is profit.

For his practice he charges £36 per session excluding VAT. That means that Shaun would need to conduct 70 sessions to make this back. We approximate that each client will come for an average of 5 sessions. Based on this formula Yell Products have to generate 14 clients per year to pay for themselves. When one looks at that, it is easy to see that one does not need to gain many clients from this medium in order to recoup a reasonable investment.

How much you need to invest depends on what you wish to achieve and the nature of the competition in your area. When one of the authors (Fiona) first qualified as a counsellor there was no other named counsellor advertising in her local Yellow Pages. Therefore a comparatively small advert was exceedingly effective. If she had had a half page ad, she would have had very few extra clients. Now, however, there are many and so to gain the same number of referrals as she had before she would need to increase her advert size accordingly.

If it is your intention to earn a full time living from your therapy, you need to be serious about your advertising investment. Most therapies are a competitive business and there are likely to be plenty of therapists who are prepared to invest more with the intention to make their presence dwarf yours. Remember the old expression, you have to speculate to accumulate, so even if you are a newly qualified practitioner, invest in Yell wisely.

Size of Advertisement:

This will vary dependent on the amount you are prepared to spend. Shaun takes a Double ¼ One Colour on White Knock Out. This gets him noticed nicely. It is large enough to get attention but not too large as to be considered garish or over the top. Size of advertisement will also be dependent on your area. If you are in a catchment with a very few of your specialism, you can advertise much smaller and get the same result as a person who has to advertise large in a catchment with many pages of therapists like you.

As a little aside here, we recommend that if you have a free line advertisement in Yell, in addition to your paid ad, you place the free line in a different category (if there is one that is suitable). It is a waste of resources to have the freebie there with the paid. Categories such as stress management, therapists, clinics, or complementary therapies may be appropriate and by doing so you are increasing your exposure in the book.

What To Put In:

This part could almost be called what not to put in. It is obvious that a practitioner wants to put in his/her advertisement all of the relevant details about themselves and their qualifications. We have heard many different arguments about whether to put designating letters after one's name or not and we have determined that those who do get a better response than those who don't. However, do not over do it. If the authors put all of the letters they are entitled to after their names the list of letters would take up half a sheet of A4. People are not impressed by this, they are sceptical of it.

Use degree and diploma qualifications and main memberships / fellowships. Also avoid putting in anything that could be construed as making claims of being medically qualified, if you are not. This is extended in that therapists should not be using diagnostic terminology in their advertising unless your brand of therapy specifically allows this. The Advertising Standards Authority is quite right in insisting that all claims made by practitioners be open to scrutiny and that if a claim is made that cannot be justified, it is not to be advertised. Also, unless one has appropriate medical credentials one should not advertise medical conditions that therapy can help with. This whole issue can be avoided by simply refraining from using "Laundry Lists" in advertising. A laundry list is a full listing of all of the potential issues a particular therapy has been known to be effective in treating. This is a risky strategy in that if someone lists something that they have had no experience in a client could argue that the practitioner misled them.

Remember, people who are looking in Yellow Pages are probably already clear about what it is that they want, if they weren't they would not be looking. So as an advertiser all you need is to explain your particular service and that should be sufficient.

We are sure you can see that Yellow Pages is an effective means of advertising and marketing, but it must be used with discretion and good judgement to make it pay for you.

It's important to make your product look good

More on Advertising

What are the other options for advertising one's therapy practice? The main places for a practitioner to advertise are the Internet (see p122), newspapers, specialist publications, and other miscellaneous areas.

Newspapers

Newspapers may seem the most logical place for a new or experienced practitioner to advertise. After all, the paper comes out either daily or weekly so there is no reason to have to wait for a whole year as you may have to do when you are dealing with Yellow Pages. Bearing this in mind, newspaper advertising is by and large the most expensive form of advertising on a long-term basis. If one considers that a weekly advertisement can cost upwards of £30-£50 per insertion for even a lineage advertisement on a 50 week year one can see the costs involved. Also one must also consider whether the paper is going to attract the type of clientele that a therapist would like. As non PC as this may be, therapy is still a pursuit of the educated middle classes as opposed to the working class members of the public. (There are exceptions to this generalisation of course).

Therefore, is the paper that you are going to choose to advertise in going to attract the type of person you wish to attract? The authors over the years have tried a variety of newspaper advertisements in a variety of types of publication, and have found the results at best to be hit and miss. It also seems to vary geographically, maybe related to the distribution of a newspaper. For example Fiona found the local paper in Exeter to be consistently effective, and the papers in her current area in rural Leicestershire to be completely the opposite. However in Exeter there was one daily paper, whereas in her current location there are two, neither being specifically for her closest town.

If you want to explore the use of newspaper advertising, there are some hints that you might bear in mind.

- Do not take the price proposed as being set in stone. Most advertising sales people make their money on getting the highest commission possible for the advertisement. This means the more expensive the ad, the better the commission. The truth is that there is a tremendous amount of flexibility as to how much an advertisement will cost. We recommend that when you enquire, and you get a price, you tell the sales person that the cost cannot be justified and that you will have to reconsider. It is almost a guarantee that within an hour that sales person will come back to you after speaking with his "manager" or "supervisor" with a much more attractive offer.

- If your practice is more established and you are looking for occasional advertising, you can ask if the paper has "remnant ads". A remnant advertisement is an ad that get put into the paper when there is a space that needs to be filled. This rate is generally much more favourable as your advertisement will not appear every week.

- In newspaper advertising, less is definitely more. What we mean here is that one does not have to write an epic in order to get a response. Remember, there are very few people who will approach you for therapy, who do not have some idea that what you do is going to be of some benefit to them. If you state too much in your advertisement you are more likely to put people off, because if you say you treat 20 conditions, and the potential client has condition 21, they are more likely than not to go to someone else, because you have limited yourself by mentioning everything other than what the client wanted.

- Please avoid using a photograph in your newspaper advertisement (regardless of the points made on p108). No one looks good in newsprint, so avoid it. A picture can just as easily put someone off as to make them want to book with you.

- Boxing is a sport (and that's debatable) not an advertising necessity. Many advertising sales people will tell you that having a box advertisement in a newspaper is better than having lineage. In one sense this is true, it is better for the newspaper sales person because it costs you more. There is no verifiable evidence that a box in a newspaper is any better than lineage. In fact, often because of space issues, a box is placed where there is space, not necessarily where your advertisement would attract the clients who are interested in your services. One of the only advertisements Shaun uses is in City Life Magazine in Manchester (more on this type of publication in a moment) He runs a lineage advertisement in this publication on a weekly basis which costs £112.80 per annum. This advertisement regularly generates 2-5 new bookings per month. The advertisement reads simply:

Hypnotherapy Consultations, caring professional service, qualified and registered practitioner, free brochure available Shaun Brookhouse, PhD, DCH, FNCH, 0161 881 1677 www.hypno-nlp.com

- Use the word free if you can (free brochure is ideal) as it is well known in the advertising world that this word has a huge drawing power

- A technique you could utilise whether you take out a box or a lineage advert is something referred to as a Haemorrhoid Treatment Advertisement. If a person skimming the newspaper not particularly looking for therapeutic treatment and comes across the word **Haemorrhoids** and he himself suffers with them, he is more likely than not to want to read your advertisement. A person takes on average 3-8 minutes to read through a newspaper. That means that your advert only has a matter of seconds to attract the person's attention. The Haemorrhoid Treatment ads can get people's attention quickly. By doing this we are not necessarily stating we are specialising in it, but by listing an eye catching banner of a condition we will likely get the potential client to stop and at least consider our service as opposed to the person who sees a banner of the therapy and thinks "I don't need/believe in XXXXXX"

- If you choose a lineage ad, you need to check the specialist sections in the newspaper concerned. The authors have had different experiences of this issue. Years ago, Shaun ran an advertisement in the Manchester Evening News, and at that time there was no specialist counselling, psychotherapy or hypnotherapy section, so the advertisement was run in the "Personal" section. Whilst the practice did receive a lot of calls, none of them were for therapy. However, Fiona used this section in the Exeter local paper with great success (and only a couple of dodgy responses). Her theory is that people look at this section out of curiosity and so you may attract those who were not actively looking for you!

Specialist Publications

There are two types of specialist publication that we will be looking at, trade type publications and what's on type publications. Trade type publications would include things like "Positive Health" or "Here's Health". Basically, these publications cater to a market of people who have an interest in complementary and alternative treatments. The difficulty with these types of publications is that they are national and that there is still a bias in the securing of therapeutic services for a client to seek a local practitioner first.

It is of course possible for you to attract a local or even a national market in these types of magazines. However, it is important to realise that these publications charge what could be considered by many to be over the odds for their advertising space simply because they are glossy. When deciding whether to advertise in this type of publication it is important to be aware how much business this will have to generate to pay for itself. This was discussed in the Yellow Pages Section, but it is even more relevant here. This is due to the fact that these publications have a month long shelf life, therefore if you do not continually advertise in these publications it is unlikely that you will be "discovered" in back editions.

These types of publications are better served to persons offering either training courses or courses of therapy. This is not to say that these publications are not a credible place to advertise, it is just that you might have to spend more time and money to get a reasonable return than you might be prepared to.

The second type of specialty publication is the "XXX Life Magazine". That is to say magazines that are about lifestyle as opposed to news or any specific subject. Publications like "City Life" or "Cheshire Life" fall into this type of classification. These publications can be an excellent source of new business because more often than not they are purchased by persons who have reasonable disposable earnings.

It goes without saying that you are not likely to be interested in the latest film or restaurant if you are having trouble paying the gas bill. Persons who buy these publications also fall into the "Educated Middle Class" that we mentioned earlier, so these are the sorts of clients that we as therapists are looking for. There are however, a couple of points to watch out for. As many of these types of publications are what one would consider to be "Glossies" their cost for advertising is greater than newspapers, and also, they are often not as flexible when it comes to negotiation as newspapers can be.

Also, one should be advertising in the appropriate area, in other words places like Manchester border Lancashire, Cheshire and Yorkshire. This type of publication tends to be "geographic centric" in that readers of these publications tend to want to see a "local therapist". Just make sure that you are local to the publication you are using and it should be fine.

Miscellaneous Areas

These types of publication seem to have no commonality except that you would not have head of them unless you were cold called by one of their sales staff. Hardly a week goes by when we are not offered a spectacular opportunity to throw our money away. "I represent the local GP Practice" or "I am calling on behalf of XXXX Hospital" or "We are compiling a diary for the Fire Service" are common introductions these types of publications will use.

As a rule of thumb consider this, if a person has to ring to tell you how great their product is, it probably isn't. Consider that for Newspapers, Magazines, and even Yellow Pages, the onus is on you the practitioner to contact them not the other way around. We teach our students that if advertisers have to cold call you give them the cold shoulder. These types of advertisements promise high returns for a comparatively high investment. We advise you to avoid these publications as there are better and less expensive ways to advertise your professional services.

If you do decide to advertise in one of these publications do ensure that you read all the small print. Fiona was caught out by a contract which committed her to paying for two editions of a directory which was never published and Shaun was tricked into paying for advertising up front which did not materialise until two years later! That was £1000 each thrown away. Please learn from our expensive mistakes! Also, be sceptical of offers of exclusivity and get that in writing or it will be your word against theirs.

A final note on print advertising: it is the most often used and most often badly used form of advertising. Always make sure that someone else proofreads your advertisement, it is easy to hallucinate what you think you see rather than what is there in reality. Make sure there is a response mechanism for your ad (ie phone number, address, email address or any combination of the three).

The Internet

However you feel about the Internet and technology in general, the Internet is here to stay and will become more and more important as a resource for more and more of the population. If you are not on-line YOU ARE MISSING OUT. We cannot emphasise enough how vital an Internet presence is for your business. For example, one of the authors (Shaun) gets a minimum of 8 new clients a month from the Internet, the most he has had is 20 new clients in a single month just from the Internet.

Here are some hints and tips for having a successful Internet site, as of March 2003, Shaun's main practice site (www.hypno-nlp.com) receives in excess of 20,000 hits per month. Does that mean he gets 20,000 bookings? No of course not. However, it is essential that for your website to generate business, you need to get the hits.

Domain name

This is one of the most important aspects of your site. The domain name should be reasonably short; people will not remember www.manchesterhypnotherapistnamedshaunbrookhouse.com When he first purchased a domain name he wanted it to cover the two main aspects of his practice (hypnosis and NLP) so he came up with hypno-nlp as the best description. Look at the work you want to do and find a descriptive phrase that you can incorporate into a good domain name. Once you have done this, you need to purchase as many variations of this name as possible so that people won't steal your name.

For example with hypno-nlp, Shaun owns all the top level domain names, plus all but one secondary domain name. That is to say, he owns .com, .net, .org, .co.uk, .org.uk, .biz, .info, and he allowed a graduate of his to purchase .me.uk.

All but her address point to Shaun's website so if you type in any of these variations you will find him. If you have a reasonably well known name in your field of therapy you can go for yourname.com. This is an easy way for people to find you even if they do not know your domain name. Please do not leave this to chance, the domain name is a cheap way of easily getting your name about. Having an isp address like www.yahoo.co.uk/hypnosis/steve/htm looks and is unprofessional and again, like the earlier example, will not be remembered by anyone.

To get a domain name, you will need to check whether it has been taken already, and then (if not) you can buy it on-line. A good site for this is www.nic.uk.

Once you have your domain name organised put it on all your advertising. Even on your voice mail. It will instil confidence in your clients and give you an air of permanence. Of course, it also gives them the opportunity to find out more about you.

Your site

Setting up a website is easy. Firstly you need to must rent some space on the Internet from an Internet Service Provider, who will host their domain name, web pages and provide e-mail services. If you want to create your own site you can use templates, or a full programming tool such as Dreamweaver. However, if you don't want to attempt this, there are plenty of ways of getting your site created for you. a simple approach is to contact a reputable web development company and have them take care of the Domain Registration, hosting, web design and e-mail. We have negotiated a deal for our readers with Learntech who developed the site for the National Council for Hypnotherapy (www.hypnotherapists.org.uk). (For contact details see p165)

Design of your site is all important; it needs to be laid out to maximise the amount of time people will spend there and to ensure that they get the information they came for. We recently saw a therapist's website that did not give the therapists name, details of the type of therapy or any other information that could help you choose whether to visit her. It did contain some nice pictures and poetry, and a phone number to call. We doubt it will be achieving its purpose.

It is important that the site be both pleasing to the eye and simple to navigate. All too often businesses have very complicated sites developed and people do not stay on them long enough for all of the graphics to download. This is because, whilst Internet design has moved on, the average computer has not and speed is of the essence when looking at a site. If you do not get your message across in seconds, a potential client will move on to another site which does. Keep your graphics simple and consistent. You may choose to have a photo of your self on the site (see p108). People buy therapists not therapy and in a highly visual medium like the Internet, it can be important to let your clients "see you are okay" before they are likely to book. Whether or not you choose to use a photo, ensure your name is prominent. You do not want your potential clients to have to search for your identity.

Content is equally important of course, and in this medium you can cater for those who want to read a little and those who want to read a lot quite easily. However, it is important not to put anybody off with the information you provide. Of course, you cannot please all the people all the time, but there are some definite things you can avoid. For example, there is a fad for mail order ordinations at the moment. You might well have very strong religious convictions, but advertising yourself on line as "the Rev or Rt Rev such and such" is likely to put more people off than turn them on to your services. Also, things like "spiritual healing", "past life regression", and other forms of fringe type interventions can also put people off. From our experience, if people want these things they will ask you rather than you having to announce it. If you really want to advertise these services, set up an additional website to cover these interventions separate from your main practice site.

Complexity can be built into your site as you progress. For example you may choose to add a forum for people to leave questions for answering, weekly news items, frequently asked questions or a shop for any merchandise that you may sell.

Email

There is no point in having a website, no matter how wonderful, if you do not answer your emails. The President of the National Guild of Hypnotists in the US jokes that as he types Dear Shaun in his email, he already has a reply from him saying yes. Emails must be treated like voice mail and answered within a couple of hours at the latest from receipt. Whilst this will not always be possible, one should be using this as a goal. Clients want to feel as though they are being valued, and one of the best ways to do this is to reply promptly to their queries.

Email is a relatively new form of communication and people use it differently. There are few conventions, but we would suggest that you:

- Write fairly formally
- Avoid fancy graphics
- Avoid standard email abbreviations such as btw and imho
- Be careful with humour as tone can be misinterpreted

Search engines

Once all this is done, you need to get your site listed with the main search engines and get the best possible position. One way to do this is to pay one of the numerous companies that spam your email box to do this for you. Some of these services may well be good, but we would rather attend to these things ourselves. We have found some excellent submission and positioning software from Apex Pacific called Dynamic Submission. However there are many other software houses which do this sort of thing for a fraction of the cost of paying someone to do it for you. Additionally, one of the best ways to get search engine positioning, is to ensure that your site appears on as many other sites as possible. You do this by asking the owner of the site in question to have a link from his/her site to yours. Shaun's practice site is currently linked to over 300 other sites world wide, which is why his site appears high in the search engines.

It is important that your site has as much information on the things you do in it as possible. The spiders which search your site for the search engines are looking for text, so have your key words match up with the sort of things that a person might type into a search engine in order to find you. Also, be as descriptive as possible about the services you provide in the main body of your website, because the spiders search there too. So if a person types in a specific condition that appears somewhere in your site, you stand a chance of your site being listed in the search engine enquiry that person makes.

The Internet gives you the opportunity to cast your net wider than your local community. We sincerely urge you to do this. We have had many clients over the years from different areas including foreign countries, who would not have found us except for our web presence. This is a golden opportunity for you to gain a wider market, whilst maintaining a professional appearance.

On-line directories

There are numerous on-line directories in all health-related fields. You can search for these using an Internet search engine, but here are a few possibilities that you can look into:

www.healthypages.co.uk
www.netdoctor.co.uk
www.uktherapists.com
www.selfgrowth.com
www.synergy-health.co.uk
www.chisuk.org.uk

Lecturing

Giving public talks is great way to generate interest in your practice FREE (or nearly free). People who attend therapy are often interested on an intellectual level in the work that we do, in addition to realising that we can help them to change. Clients will do their research before coming to see you, but would it not be nice to be able to have them see you before they come for therapy, so that they know that you are the right therapist for them?

For some therapists, the free consultation is the way to do this. We are, generally speaking, opposed to the free consultation for several reasons. The first is that often clients will be expecting some form of therapy at this session, and when they do not receive it, they leave disappointed and disillusioned. Also, as busy practitioners it will become more and more difficult for you to arrange the time to do free consultations. They tend to clog up the appointment book. Finally, there are clients who abuse the good-natured therapist who is prepared to perhaps give a little extra in these consultations. We have heard stories about clients who have seen a dozen or more therapists using the free consultation session as a way of receiving therapy.

Put yourself on display

Public talks are a great way to achieve some of the outcomes of the free initial consultation with you being in control of the process. Let us look at the sort of thing one would be able to present. Some therapies lend themselves better to this type of promotion than others, for example it would be quite easy for hypnotherapists to do entertaining public talks because they can incorporate a demonstration or two into the presentation, and the public have a natural fascination with hypnosis. It may be a harder task for a reflexologist for example. The first most important thing for the public talk is to find the right title. People will not bother to attend if the title does not attract their interest.

For example:

"Counselling: a person centred approach to therapy"

would probably not be as effective a title as:

"Counselling: the way to get the life you want and deserve!"

Admittedly, the second title may not sit comfortably with some practitioners but it is important to note that there is very little point in preparing to do a talk if no one attends. So the title is very important. Some other titles one could consider are:

"Hypnotise your way to better health"
"Your future is through your feet"
"Coaching, the new way to achieve success in your life"
"Achieve your personal development goals through psychotherapy"
"The power of pong"
"Brief therapy....long term solutions"
"How to say Bye Bye to Bad Backs"

You can, of course, come up with your own ideas for the best title for you and your therapy. It is important to note that the title must not promise what it cannot deliver. The authors recently attended a weekend seminar which promised a list of 12 outcomes, none of which were covered by the end of the weekend. That is a guaranteed way to turn off your audience.

Titles also should not make claims of treatment. We say this, because in some cases people will attend a public talk in order to receive therapy there and then. It would be unethical for you to provide therapy in this way as well as impractical. Any demonstrations should be kept simple.

The next issue one needs to consider is where to hold such a talk. We would recommend that one holds it at the local public library. There are several reasons for this. The first is that provided the presentation that you are giving is free, you can get a room at the library free. Libraries are there to serve the public interest and public talks are in that interest. This is an important point to remember, these talks are free of charge to attend. This will get you more attendees, as well as showing you to be a publicly spirited practitioner. By having a free presentation at the library, the library will also be able to promote it without charge, both in the library and in the "What's On" section of the local newspaper.

So you have your venue and title, the next issue is what should you include in your presentation. As previously stated some therapies lend themselves better to presentations than others, but consider the following outline for a 60 minute presentation:

Introduction: In this part of the presentation you outline the therapy in general terms. What is its history? What is it useful in treating? Who uses it? (Famous persons for example), How does it work? At this point as well, if your therapy is something that you can demonstrate, 5-10 minutes of demonstration at this point would be useful.

Specifics About You: At this point of the presentation, you can discuss the specifics about you and your practice. Mention qualifications, experiences, personal anecdotes at this point of the presentation. (10 Minutes)

Questions and Answers: This is arguably the most important part of the presentation. It will give you an idea of what your audience is looking for and what their motives were for attending your presentation. At this point you can give specific information as to how your therapy will be able to assist them. (Minimum of 20 Minutes)

We consider 60 minutes to be the optimum time for such a presentation. Most practitioners can talk about what they do in an entertaining and informative manner for an hour. Also, it is an easy amount of time for the audience to slot in without having to make special arrangements. Finally, it is about the length of time the average person can give you their attention (as long as you keep it interesting and varied).

There are certain things that you should bring with you for this presentation. The most important is some form of brochure. People like to have something to take away with them, especially as the presentation is free or charge, it gives them a greater feeling of value. Your practice brochure should be on every seat in the room. We have experimented with having the brochures at the front and the back of the room, and we have found that often when brochures need to be collected, the people who collect them are often the people who do not need to consult you. It is often the people with the real issues who are too shy or embarrassed to collect a brochure, so the very people you need to be reaching are not reached. Having a brochure on the chair of everyone, means that everyone is treated equally and therefore there is no shame in leaving with a brochure.

You might have some form of product with you for sale at the end of the presentation. If you opt to do this, make sure that the product is relevant to the talk you just gave. For example, having crystals for sale at a coaching talk is probably not appropriate, but having self-hypnosis tapes at a talk on hypnosis would be. Please do not hawk your product, just tell people that the item(s) are available at the end of the presentation. It is preferable that when you do a talk you have a friend attend with you to take care of the sale of these items. You want to be available to talk to anyone who wants to talk to you rather than being weighed down being a sales clerk.

Finally, you might want to have a basic hand-out of what you talked about. Very often people like to review what they have learned in the form of notes. By giving this type of hand-out, it means that for the hour they can give you their undivided attention rather than worrying about taking the appropriate notes. These hand-outs MUST have your practice details in a prominent position on them, as these will also act as marketing material.

If you have a website, It is recommended that you have a special "appearances" section which is where you can do a little promotion of the talks that you do. By doing this you are setting yourself out still further as the expert X in your area.

These talks also have another use. Rather than simply doing them for the public, you can do them for service clubs such as Rotary or the Women's Institute. These clubs provide a public service and often look for speakers to address their meetings. It is a marvellous way to network and to secure further business for your practices.

The media

Writing

Writing is one of the most useful ways to gain a reputation in the field which will pay dividends in the long run. When one looks at writing, there are three separate areas to consider:

1. People writing about you,
2. You writing about yourself,
3. You publishing professionally for your profession.

People writing about you

Getting editorial space in a worthwhile publication, is a far better means of getting new business than most other forms of paid advertisement. Many years ago, one of the authors (Shaun) had an article written which has generated for his practice to date over £20,000 in revenue with at least that same amount being referred out to other practitioners. The way this occurred, was that Shaun wrote to the editor of a national health magazine asking if they wanted a monthly column on hypnosis. He never heard from her but two years later she became a freelancer, writing an article on successful hypnotherapy for Zest Magazine. Shaun provided her with a willing client's case history and left it at that. He received a phone call at 7:30am the morning of the publication coming out and discovered that not only had the magazine come out, but the article was also published in full in one of the National newspapers.

You writing about yourself

Some practitioners get great success by producing a practice newsletter. In this one would include things like new therapies on offer, awards, upgrades in professional memberships, granting of new qualifications, etc. It should never include testimonials, as these are viewed to be unprofessional (see p139). Also, one would probably produce this every couple of months as producing something like this on a monthly basis would be very difficult. Additionally, some publications will provide you with editorial space if you take out advertising with them. We would suggest that you have a set piece, either written by you or a good copyrighter and use this whenever the media would like information about you and your practice.

Publishing professionally for your profession

This serves a much different purpose to popular publication. When one publishes for the profession, it serves to give the impression of clinical and professional expertise. The authors publish widely, both for professional publications and the popular media. Clients will not come directly from professional publications, but they can and often do as referrals from other professionals who see you as being an expert in your field.

Radio and television

Radio and television are considered by many to be an excellent way to get the word out about your practice. In some cases this is absolutely true and in others not.

When looking at radio and television one must consider the programme one is going to appear on. Shaun has had experience being on a number of television and radio programmes, with mixed results.

As a general rule, the later the programme, (especially on radio) the better. For some years Shaun appeared on a local radio programme which went out at around midnight. The programme was general, but Shaun would be the guest when the topic was phobia and anxiety. Shaun appeared on this programme 3 times and each time at 1am the practice phone began to ring and did so until around 4am. The reason for this was that the listeners were generally in discomfort and therefore were up, in many cases, unable to sleep because their problem had become so great. By being available to take these calls at a time when people were at their lowest, Shaun managed to maximise the effect of appearing on the programme.

Shaun also appeared on a popular BBC morning programme. The topic was hypnosis, and it was felt that his being there would enhance the reputation of both clinical hypnosis and his practice. The programme was good for hypnosis but a missed opportunity for Shaun as the producers would not let him mention his own practice, claiming that it breached BBC guideline (this claim was later to prove false).

When appearing on radio or television it is important for the therapist to know certain things:

- What is the show's angle and what is it attempting to accomplish?

- How much time will you get to put your views forward?

- If there is no speakers fee, will the producers allow a professional "plug" for your practice?

- Will the general public be able to participate?

Knowing these things will help you to make your media appearances successful, not only in terms of your practice, but also in terms of your profession as a whole.

Generating referrals

The US marketing expert, Elsom Eldrige, EdM(Harvard), states that approximately 25% of your previous clients will either return for additional therapeutic services or refer someone to you. We concur with this figure and it has certainly shown itself to be true in our own practices. The topic for this section is to look at the five criteria for successful referral generation from ex or existing clients.

The important thing to bear in mind here is that it is as unprofessional to pester a client for referrals as it is to pay or induce clients to refer friends and family to see you. There is a professional way to do this which has integrity at its root. The first of these criteria is that the client doing the referring should have been successful in their treatment with you. Although it is not without precedence, it should be assumed that the client who has not been successful will be unlikely to tell his or her friends about how wonderful a therapist you are.

The next criterion is rapport. This is very important within the therapeutic relationship but it is possible that there are some therapists who manage to assist their clients to a successful resolution of their issues, without really managing to achieve good rapport with the client in question. So even if the client is successful with their treatment, it is again unlikely that this person will refer if the individual did not have a good rapport with you.

Being comfortable with you is not the only issue that has to be overcome in order to have clients refer to you, the client needs to be comfortable with therapy itself. This is an equal concern no matter what discipline you practice. Here in the UK and in other areas of the world, there is still a misconception about attending therapy as meaning that you are weak and that you should be able to pull yourself together without professional intervention. A client should be guided to feel comfortable with the therapy you practice. How relevant this factor is will depend on your branch of therapy. For example osteopathy would have less of a problem here than hypnotherapy. Let us look at the following fictitious client.

Jane has lost weight with hypnotherapy(criterion: success) and has had good rapport with you as her therapist (criterion: rapport). She meets friends whom she has not seen for a time, and they comment on her astounding weight loss. When asked how she did it she replies "Will power, it was tough but I managed to do it".

Of course we understand that Jane did have to make effort to lose the weight but she has not mentioned the fact that she had professional help in doing so. This more often than not is because of a feeling of shame that is associated with seeking professional help. One of the most important jobs of the therapist is to assist clients in feeling more comfortable with the treatment they are receiving.

A socially skilled client is the next criterion. Even when these first three criteria are met, it is unlikely that the client will be in a position to refer, if they lack social skills and contacts. Let us use Jane again:

Jane has lost weight with hypnotherapy (criterion: success) and has good rapport with you (criterion: rapport) and she is happy to tell the world about hypnotherapy and HER hypnotherapist (criterion: comfort). Jane works in a one person office. Since losing weight she has opted to bring her own lunch to the office rather than going to the local sandwich shop for lunch. She spends her weekend doing household chores and looking after her pets.

Now despite the fact that the first three criteria are met, it would appear that Jane does not have the outlet to tell people about you. The final criterion is probably the most obvious: one needs to ask for the referral. That is to say ask professionally and once. Let us look at Jane again.

Jane has lost weight with hypnotherapy (criterion: success) and has good rapport with you (criterion: rapport) and she is happy to tell the world about hypnotherapy (criterion: comfort). Jane is the captain of the local ladies golf team and spend a great deal of her time at social functions and charity events (criterion: social skill). At a chance meeting in town, she makes another appointment to see you for a bit of extra work. Upon her arrival she says "I feel so much better after seeing you, and that I am so keen on what hypnotherapy has done for me I am sending all my friends to Mr X (another hypnotherapist)

Now you might well think that this is odd as all of the other criteria had been met, and yet Jane has opted to refer her considerable social circle to a different therapist. When one enquires, Jane says, *"I would have sent them to you, but I assumed that as you were so good you would not have the time to see new clients and that you would not want to be bothered".* Odd as this might seem it is not uncommon. Some clients will not refer people to you because they think they are doing you a favour. So it is important to ask for the referral. As we previously said, this should be done only once and in a professional manner like this *"When people see how well you are doing, your recommendation would be appreciated"* By doing this you let them know that you would welcome any referrals without sounding desperate or pushy.

These criteria are not exhaustive, but more often than not if they are followed, your ex and current clients will fill your appointment book week in and week out.

Use of testimonials

Whether the use of testimonials is considered acceptable will depend on the therapy that you are offering. If you are unsure, please check with your professional body.

In general terms, we do not believe that the use of testimonials is an ethical practice, nor that it makes good business sense. The exception to this would be in a field where it is normal to use them and potential clients would actively be discouraged if you did not.

Our reasons for our stance are as follows:

- Traditional medicine in the UK does not involve the use of testimonials, nor does psychology
- Testimonials prove nothing as they can be faked
- There is always a risk of breaking confidentiality by showing, say, a letter from a client, even if their name and address have been erased
- If a client gives permission they may change their mind later, and may not have thought through the possibilities of what might happen if friends or family see what they have written.

Other ideas

Offer discounts to members of sports or health clubs

If appropriate for your therapy and training, offer to give talks at schools. Hand out brochures.

Use yourself and your car as an advertising medium. Wendi Friesen put a sign in her car saying "Hypnogolf" when she went to watch a tournament: she got two new clients! You could even get a baseball hat giving the name of your therapy.

Talk loudly about what you do whenever there are people around, and have business cards ready. This idea will not fit comfortably with some, as usual this is a matter of choice. We know of someone who does this and just succeeds in sounding arrogant, so be careful.

Target special interest groups or specific types of company. Don Mottin runs stress management classes specifically for hairdressers or taxi drivers. The class is the same but they feel they are special.

Produce tapes with a brief introduction to your therapy and give them out as you would business cards.

Write newsletters and post to current and ex clients.

Send a thank you note to a client for a referral, but only when you've checked that is ok with your new client!

Target your marketing to fit with "National Days". Contact special interest groups for the areas in which you work and find out what they are planning that you can tie into.

*M*aintaining standards

Ethics

You may have noticed that the title of this book includes the word "ethical". We like to think that this will be important to you, but we have seen many examples of unethical behaviour on the part of therapists; some intentional but mostly through lack of thought.

So, we would strongly urge you to

Read your code of ethics!

Of course, by saying this we are presuming that you belong to a professional society. If you do not, please join. The professional society for your therapy can be one of the best resources you have for building a successful practice. Here are just some of the reasons for belonging:

- Many societies operate a referral service so you could easily recoup your investment directly
- Most have a journal or newsletter to help you keep up to date with developments in your field
- Many run seminars and conferences which also help you to keep up to date and develop
- Societies provide a network of like minded people
- Societies offer advice on any therapy related issues
- Many have corporate advertising schemes, for example in the Yellow Pages
- Many have deals for competitive rates of insurance
- You can be involved in the decision making process for your therapy (eg regulation processes)
- Your potential clients will see you as having greater credibility

Ethical issues will vary from therapy to therapy, but here are some considerations that will apply to all:

Client Welfare

The welfare of the client is the primary concern of the therapist. It should only take second place if not to do so would seriously jeopardise other members of the public or the therapist's welfare.

Confidentiality

Confidentiality is to be maintained in all but the most exceptional circumstances. These can only include: legal action (criminal or civil court cases where a court order is made demanding disclosure - includes coroner's courts) and where there is good cause to believe that not to disclose would cause danger of serious harm to others. Most standards of confidentiality applied in professional contexts are based on the Common Law concept of confidentiality where the duty to keep confidence is measured against the concept of "greater good". A stronger form (as we would suggest), may be provided by the use of a written contract containing a confidentiality clause. The sharing of anonymous case histories with supervisors and peer-support groups is not a breach of professional confidentiality. The sharing of open case histories with supervisors is also not a breach. Feedback to referring medical practitioners can take the form of general comments as to progress; specific details should be kept confidential.

Service

Therapists will only offer services in areas in which they have demonstrated their competence, to the agreed level for their therapy. They have a responsibility to provide the client with the best possible service available even to the extent of onwards referral to another therapist or medical practitioner that may offer such a service.

Development of 'Skill-base'

Therapists are required to maintain or improve their level of skills and professional competence by:

a. undertaking formal continuing training, by attending workshops, courses and seminars, of an standard approved for their therapy, AND

b. sharing experiences and exploring such with supervisors/peer-support groups

They should also maintain an awareness of research and developments in their field and other linked fields.

Exploitation

All exploitation is abuse.

Therapists shall not behave in any manner that shall give rise to the exploitation of a client. They shall not enter into any other relationship, outside the professional/therapeutic relationship, while treating a client. They shall make their charges known to the client before therapy is commenced. They shall terminate therapy at the earliest time, commensurate with the good care and continuing welfare of the client. They shall not accept any inappropriate gifts, gratuities or favours from a client.

Advertising

Advertising, no matter in what form or medium it is placed, shall represent a true picture of the therapist, their skill base, qualifications, facilities and any benefits that may be expected from hypnosis and shall conform to current Advertising Law.

General Conduct

Therapists shall not behave in any manner, within or outside the context of therapy, that would undermine the public's confidence in the profession or bring the profession into disrepute. This includes a failure to act appropriately when they become aware of another therapist's unethical activity, improper use of therapy, criminal conviction, misbehaviour towards other Health or Social Care professionals, discrimination on the basis of ethnic or sexual factors or anything that is the subject of any civil judgement regarding neglect of duty of care. They are obliged to advise clients of appropriate avenues of complaint.

Professional Indemnity Insurance

This is a prerequisite for any therapist to practice and must be maintained by the practitioner. It is recommended that it should be an agreed adequate minimum cover.

Provision of a Contract

All therapy is undertaken as a result of a contract between the client and the therapist. It is preferable that this should not be an oral contract which is loose and open to abuse and misinterpretation or dispute. It should preferably be a written contract. Such a contract should include statements of cost per session or whole course of therapy, confidentiality, the client's right of access to the complaints procedure of the professional society and the fact that there can be no guarantee of a 'cure'. The inclusion of a clause that defines the scope of confidentiality, within therapy raises it from a Common Law duty to Contractual Limitation and duty to deliver. (Thus it becomes easier for all parties to understand their rights and duties within the therapeutic relationship and lowers any risk of abuse or misunderstanding.)

Other issues

Individual therapies may also have clauses relating to

- Supervision (see p147)
- Display of credentials and testimonials (see p139)
- Note taking and retention
- Recording of sessions
- Treatment of children
- Hygiene
- Facilities

So check out your code, and keep up to date with changes, because, simply put, being ethical will help you to be truly successful.

Continuing Professional Development

Many professional societies specify a requirement that therapists continue to take courses, and some specify a minimum number of hours or days per year. However, it is by no means universal that this is adhered to. The authors have heard therapists say such things as "there is nothing I need to learn", or "I don't have time".

So let's make two statements which we firmly believe and hope that you will accept:

There is always something to learn which can benefit you and your clients

You have time to learn

It is amazing arrogance to suggest that no one has anything to teach you. Even if you are the world's greatest expert on one thing, there will always be new angles, and related topics that you can learn about and which can improve your service.

Time is often an issue for all of us. We recently heard a comment suggesting that therapists who "run courses and write books obviously don't have time to see real clients". That person must have fewer hours in his week than we do, as we find this possible with a client rate of up to 30 per week. The same applies to CPD. Of course, there are other things apart from work that encroach on our time, families being perhaps the most important.

One of the authors (Fiona) trained as a therapist when her first child was less than a year old. CPD training was difficult for the first few years due to feeding him, a second pregnancy and feeding that child. You may be in a similar situation, but if you cannot travel to courses, you can still do CPD.

Keep learning!

Here is a list of possible ways of undertaking CPD:

- Higher level training (eg postgraduate courses)
- Seminars and workshops on aspects of your therapy
- Seminars and workshops on related therapies
- Conferences
- On-line learning opportunities
- Distance learning courses
- Tapes, CDs and videos
- Books

Supervision

Supervision is a relationship between two therapists, which gives the supervisee a structured support system that encourages their competency and growth through feedback, education and discussion in a safe and confidential environment.

In many branches of therapy, supervision is "for life", therefore it can be thought of as a process designed to help you to be as effective as you can be in your career. When you are just starting out, your supervisor will have partly a continued training role as they share their experience with you. You will be able to share your concerns, doubts and gaps in knowledge, as well as the joy of your successes!

When first becoming involved in a therapy that advocates supervision, it can be difficult to understand the need for it. It may seem as just another drain on your resources at a time when you want to make money, not spend it!

However, supervision can be:

- Exceedingly beneficial for you
- Exceedingly beneficial for your clients
- Valuable to the profession
- A factor which has a major impact on whether or not you "make it" in this field.
- A way to make connections with other therapists.

Many newly qualified therapists have supervision with their trainer. This can be a good idea as this is likely to be someone who you trust and feel comfortable with. However, the role of supervisor is different from that of trainer, so the change may be tricky, and choosing someone different can give an alternative perspective.

Here are the important points to consider when you select your supervisor:

- Are they qualified to a high level, both as a therapist and as a supervisor?
- Do you feel safe and comfortable with them?
- Are you happy with the practical arrangements, eg timings, location/method, price?
- Do you feel that you will get all you need? After all this is what it is about.

Own therapy

The perceived need for a therapist to have had their own therapy varies greatly between therapies. For example, most counselling diplomas require their students to have 50 or so hours of therapy following the theoretical model of the course, while psychoanalysis requires much more. Other therapies may not have such fixed requirements, and may rely on practical sessions for students to experience the techniques taught.

We are firm advocates of using therapy to help sort out the issues which may interfere with your ability to run a successful practice. This covers all the elements discussed earlier in the book (beliefs, values, blocks etc). However this may mean that a therapy different from your own is more applicable.

We are often amazed to see cases of therapists who do not utilise their own skills. For example hypnotherapists who do not use self-hypnotic tools to remove blocks. So use whatever you need to get the results you need.

Reflective practice

The concept of reflective practice is one that is fairly new to the therapeutic world. It is common place in education and training. The need for therapists to be able to look objectively at what they do, to learn from it and develop is essential to practitioners remaining safe and competent. Let us look at the following case example which covers therapeutic training. Though training specific, the lessons and approach can be utilised in clinical as well as a teaching practice

Mary (name has been changed to protect the identity and confidentiality of the student) is a successful executive in a company for whom Shaun was contracted to teach NLP. The group was large and diverse. Shaun had previously met Mary on an introductory course with just three attendees. Because of the intensive format, he had not ascertained her challenges until this recent course where she had to interact much more with other students. She tended to monopolise class time by asking the same question sometimes in 3 or 4 different ways. Her approach is very ego centric in that everything must be about her specifically. Examples from other students tend to only annoy her and she takes feedback by becoming defensive and awkward. She is intellectually gifted and has a first class honours degree, and has, during the course of the programme made some sweeping generalisations regarding the "uneducated", which have offended some of those in the group. One such incident at the midway part of the course, occurred where Mary was particularly challenging where both issues of feedback and intelligence came out. As this is an experiential group, any interpersonal difficulties with the attendees could have had a detrimental effect on the learning process. Mary has also had training in group dynamics, so it would not have seemed to be unreasonable to expect that she would be aware of the effect she was having on the group.

Shaun was concerned about his reaction to Mary and with the assistance of his supervisor and through perusal of the relevant literature regarding group dynamics, the building of relationships as well as papers relating to teacher/tutor development, he was able to look at these reactions. He checked out, "Is it me or is it her?" (Eyler, 2001) As a therapist, he is acutely aware of dual process as well as transference issues (Rogers, 1967) and is aware that it is possible that Mary is challenging some of his beliefs, in that he too does sometimes need to be the centre of attention and there have been times when in jest I have been less than kind to those of lesser intelligence. It became clear, however, near the half way point of the course, other students were not finding Mary easy, and one student felt so strongly about Mary's behaviour he was planning to resign from the course.

At this point Shaun looked at the underlying group processes and realised that there was a possibility that the reactions that both he and the group were having towards Mary were part of the natural group dynamics of any class. It was clear that the group had gone through its forming phase, but he felt it was possible that the group may not have yet got through the storming stage (Webber, 1982). The characteristic of this stage of group development is that the students now work out of affection or a caring about others in a deeper, less superficial manner than before. Meaningful functional relationships should develop between members. Leadership issues are resolved through interdependent behaviour, or working with others. Tasks are accomplished by recognizing unique talents in the group, leading where appropriate and sanctioned and following where productive and necessary. As this interplay occurs, trust evolves. This trust had not yet been achieved and there still seemed to be some difficulty in who was leading the group as far as the other students were concerned. As the tutor, Shaun found this to be a particularly difficult time, as previous groups seemed to be at the norming and performing stage of the group development by this stage of the course (Webber, 1982).

It was clear that Mary's anxieties about how she was perceived by both Shaun as the tutor and the group as a whole was a major issue which needed challenge. He felt that utilising an appropriate feedback mechanism would be beneficial for not only Mary, but for the entire group (Rabow, et al 1999). When Shaun studied to be an NLP Trainer he learned a system of feedback referred to as "sandwich feedback" (James, 1998) This method of feedback was utilised throughout the trainer's training, but Shaun had not really employed it in his own trainings, except for the final evaluation discussion which he has with each student prior to completion. This method of feedback focuses on three elements:
1. What did the student do right?
2. What could the student improve upon?
3. A final positive statement as to the student's work

After each exercise, the students would pair off an privately give each this feedback and then would bring the edited points to a final group feedback. Shaun would then use this model in general terms with the group, endeavouring not to single out anyone for excessive praise or constructive feedback. This seemed to have reasonable effects on the challenge that Mary wanted to have Shaun's and the class's time monopolised with issues relating to her situation specifically rather than the situation of the group as a whole. This tendency was continually challenged by both Shaun and other members of the group. Mary's method of having the exercises as well as the class discussion revert back to her in some way was consistent with manipulator tendencies noticed in other types of group work (Dinkmeyer, 1971)

At the same time the work on group dynamics was occurring, Shaun felt that he needed to challenge Mary's issues relating to her education and intelligence in general. In the type of teaching he does, the vast majority of students fall into a fairly well educated, intelligent classification. Shaun had had no experience with problems incurred because of high intelligence. So he opted to look at this as a multi cultural issue because Mary strongly identified her intelligence and education as her identity (Sharp, 1995)

Shaun decided to challenge Mary privately about some of her overt generalisations. In a private tutorial with Mary, Shaun put it to her that her stance was prejudicial to others within her working environment, and was perceived as being insulting, even by some on the course who were highly intelligent. He used a simple surface structure metaphor relating to previous well educated people who have attended the course. Through this story, he attempted to pace and lead Mary's behaviours to an eventual outcome which would be appropriate for the group as a whole in addition to Mary specifically (Gordon, 1985). He also pointed out to her that even though one of the processes that all humans do with information is to generalise (Bandler & Grinder, 1975), it did not mean that it was acceptable to speak in a manner which through thoughtlessness would cause others offence. The result of this was an unprecedented apology from her to the whole group. She disclosed several personal issues which could very well have attributed to some of her more aggressive behaviour. Her apology seems to have been meant as since this occurred there were no more overt generalisations. In fact, the group, though able to be jocular, avoided making generalisations itself. This led to the group becoming more harmonious and being able to enter the third stage of group development performing (Webber, 1982)

This situation has been an education for Shaun as a teacher. Firstly, it made him aware that on certain occasions he would prefer for conflict to go away without any active involvement in removing it. This delayed reaction can have serious repercussions for group dynamics, and Shaun has resolved that he will, in future, keep a more close observation on potential conflict and look to resolve it as soon as is possible. Also, this incident has awakened the idea that there can be discrimination on any training courses. In this case, the discrimination was unconscious for the protagonist as well as for Shaun. By this we mean that when Mary was challenged, she was unaware of how her remarks could be taken. At first, Mary was defensive in that she made reference to a comment Shaun made about therapists being able to understand deep psychological issues without basing this statement on any appreciable research. To model the behaviour which Shaun hopes his students will undertake, he also apologised to her and the group for any offence he may have caused. Now that he has been made aware of this, he is far more careful with what he says off the cuff. Additionally, Shaun has since undertaken a workshop on working with mixed ability groups and the related group dynamics, which he found useful to make him more aware of his own unconscious attitudes. Finally, Shaun realised through this experience that people are willing to change, when challenged in an appropriate manner. Gentle challenge has its place in both therapy and in teaching.

References:

Rogers, C.R. (1967) A Therapist's View of Psychotherapy On Becoming A Person London, Constable

Bandler, R, Grinder, J (1975) Structure of Magic: A Book About Language and Therapy Vol 1 Palo Alto, California, Science and Behavior Books

Gordon, D (1985) Therapeutic Metaphors, Palo Alto, California Meta Publications

Webber, R, (1982) The Group: A Cycle From Birth to Death, New York, NTL Press

James, E.W (1998) NLP Trainer's Manual, Honolulu, Advanced Neuro Dynamics,

Dinkmeyer, D (1971) Group Counseling: Theory and Practice, New York, Peacock

Washington School of Clinical and Advanced Hypnosis (1996), Equal Opportunities Policy, Manchester, Hypno-NLP Press

Sharp, H (1995) Challenging Students to Respond to Multicultural Issues: The Case Study Approach Business Communication Quarterly v58 p28-31

Rabo, J, et al (1999) Tutoring Matters: Everything You Always Wanted to Know About How to Tutor, Pennsylvania, Temple University Press

Eyler, J (2001) Creating Your Reflection Map, New Directions in Higher Education, n114 p35-43

Reflecting on yourself, your clients and your practice

The Future

How to keep going

If you have followed the exercises in this book, you will already have a good idea of where you are going and how to get there. It is important to recognise that life does not always run smoothly. These ideas will help you to persevere:

- Adopt the belief that you are a therapist. Tie the title in with your identity
- Believe in abilities (see p62 and throughout)
- Look after yourself. Therapy is about caring for others. How can you do that if you don't look after yourself?
- Remember how effective you can be and how important that is to the lives of your clients and by extension their families, friends and society in general

Hang on in there!

- Value yourself and your role
- Keep learning. Be open to new experiences
- Remember the phrase, "there is no failure, only feedback"
- Set up a good support system and use it.
- If appropriate use your therapeutic skills on yourself
- Be open to having therapy (or coaching) yourself to overcome blocks and gain motivation
- Enjoy your successes (don't take them for granted) and learn from your mistakes
- Stay positive (glass half full…)
- Use reframing (see p157)
- Learn from your clients
- Review your goals constantly

Reframing

This technique is so useful that we have decided to make a special little section for it here.

When a practitioners are having a tough time it is essential that they can cope with the situation that they find themselves in. This process is known as reframing. This is the "behind every dark cloud there is a silver lining" scenario.

There are two types of reframe context and meaning. A context reframe might be:

> "I am having a slow week"
> Reframe: "The same time last year was about the same, it was even slower than it was now"
> Or, "this gives me time to read those Journals that have been piling up and to plan my advertising for the next quarter"

A meaning reframe would be:

> "Every time I advertise in the local paper it does not work"
> Reframe: Ask yourself, "What else could this situation mean?" or internally think of an opposite frame or a different meaning.
> Eg. The local paper is a bad place to advertise or I am learning what advertising does not work, so therefore I can learn and utilize what does work

Where to go next

The processes described in this book can be life long. Why would you ever stop setting goals, developing and growing? As your practice grows, your confidence grows and your goals will change. You can use the techniques involved here for other elements of your life. Fulfilment requires satisfaction in all areas of your life, including family, relationships, home, and work.

You may find you wish to expand your therapeutic base by adding related therapies, for example we feel it is advantageous for hypnotherapists to understand counselling skills and psychological theories.

As discussed above, if you are open to using the techniques and perhaps having therapy or coaching your horizons can continue to expand indefinitely.

As Buzz Lightyear would say

To infinity...and beyond!

Appendices

Sample Contract

Name of client:

Date:

This contract details the terms and conditions concerning our work together.

1. The agreement to work on the issues presented by the client in no way guarantees a cure.

2. The cost of the session will be £50 per hour.

3. Cancellation with less than 24 hours notice will cause the client to be liable for the full cost of the session.

4. Contact between sessions will be limited to telephone, email or letter.

5. Antisocial behaviour will cause the immediate cessation of treatment.

6. Clients have access to the complaints and discipline procedures of << your professional bodu>> at any time. They can be contacted on:

7. Confidentiality will be maintained in all but the most exceptional circumstances. These can only include: legal action (criminal or civil court cases where a court order is made demanding disclosure - includes coroners courts) and where there is good cause to believe that not to disclose would cause danger of

serious harm to the client or others. Most standards of confidentiality applied in professional contexts are based on the Common Law concept of confidentiality where the duty to keep confidence is measured against the concept of "greater good. The sharing of anonymous case histories with supervisors and peer-support groups is not a breach of professional confidentiality. The sharing of open case histories with supervisors and any referring NHS medical practitioner is also not a breach.

8. Notes of the sessions will be kept and are available to the client with reasonable notice.

Signed (client):   Name:

Signed (therapist):   Name:

Sample disclosure statement

Contact Information: *My name is Dr. Shaun Brookhouse, I can be contacted through my office at Richmael House, 25 Edge Lane, Chorlton cum Hardy, Manchester M21 9JH Tel: 0161 881 1677 E:Mail: DrB@hypno-nlp.com Internet: www.hypno-nlp.com*

Education and Training (Selected Qualifications): *I received my hypnotherapy training through the American College of Clinical Hypnosis (Diploma in Hypnotherapy), the London College of Clinical Hypnosis(Diploma in Clinical Hypnotherapy), the Centre Training School of Hypnotherapy and Psychotherapy(Diploma/Postgraduate Diploma in Hypnotherapy and Psychotherapy), and the International Hypnosis Institute(Master Practitioner of Ericksonian Hypnotherapy), The National Guild of Hypnotists (Board Certified Hypnotherapist, Certified Instructor of Hypnotherapy & Master Hypnotist). I have also been trained in Psychotherapy (UKCP Recognised Programme), Counselling (Diploma of Professional Counselling, Australian Institute of Professional Counsellors), NLP (Master Trainer, NFNLP), and Stress Management. Additionally, I am a Registered Psychotherapist with the United Kingdom Council for Psychotherapy and a Fellow of the National Guild of Hypnotists, the National HypnoPsychotherapy Council and the National Council for Hypnotherapy and I attend annual continuing education to maintain my training at a high level.*

University Education: *I hold a Master of Arts Degree in Education from Liverpool John Moores University, a Doctor of Clinical Hypnotherapy Degree from the American Institute of Hypnotherapy (California State Approved Degree), a Doctor of Philosophy Degree in Education & Health Services from Stratford International University (Wyoming State Licensed Degree) and a Certificate in Education, Manchester University (Assignments based on course of Hypnotherapy I designed and deliver)*

Note: The United Kingdom has not adopted any educational and training standards for the practise of hypnotherapy. This statement of credentials is for information purposes only. Confidentiality: I will not release any information to anyone without a written authorisation from you, except as provided by law. You have a right to be allowed access to my written record about you.

Redress: *I am a Fellow of the National Council for Hypnotherapy and practise in accordance with its Code of Ethics and Standards. If you ever have a complaint about my services or behaviour that I cannot resolve for you personally, you may contact the National Council for Hypnotherapy at PO Box 5779, Burton on the Wolds, Loughborough, LE12 5ZF, Tel: 01509 881477 for redress.*

Fees: *My fees for therapy are £40 per session and £60 for One Session Smoking Cessation, these fees include VAT at the appropriate rate. Cheques are made payable to S. Brookhouse or Brookhouse Hypnotherapy. There may be a charge for cancelled appointments not made within 24 hours of the scheduled time.*

My Approach: *I use an integrated approach of therapy, which incorporates hypnotherapy, NLP and Psychotherapy techniques to assist in therapeutic change. I use traditional, Ericksonian, and Analytical Techniques within my hypnotherapy approach.*

Client Signature: I have read this statement and understand what I have read:

Client Name (Print):

Client Signature: *Date:*

Sample GP letter

Dr Shaun Brookhouse
MA(Ed), DCH, PhD, PGDHP, BCH, CI, FRSH, FNCH
Board Certified Hypnotherapist
Richmael House, 25 Edge Lane, Chorlton cum Hardy, Manchester,
M21 9JH
Tel: 0161 881 1677 Fax: 0161 882 0376 Email: DrB@hypno-nlp.com
Internet www.hypno-nlp.com

Date

Dear Sirs:

As I am sure you are aware, the House of Lords recently made a report into the use of Complementary and Alternative Medicine in the UK. Being involved in this field, as a **Board Certified Hypnotherapist**, I naturally feel that this is significant. I am writing to you today to introduce myself and my practice to you and to see if there is any way that we could enter into a referral arrangement. My qualifications are as follows:

1. **MA Education Studies**
2. **DCH Doctorate in Clinical Hypnotherapy**
3. **PhD Psychotherapeutic Counselling**
4. **PhD Esoteric Studies**
5. **Post Graduate Diploma in Hypnotherapy and Psychotherapy**
6. **Board Certified Hypnotherapist**
7. **Certified Instructor of Hypnotherapy**
8. **Fellow of the Royal Society for the Promotion of Health**
9. **Fellow of the National Council for Hypnotherapy**

In addition to the above, I have several published articles on Hypnosis and Hypnotherapy and was recently voted into the International Hypnosis. All of these details can be verified at your discretion. I would very much like enter into a referral arrangement with your practice. Enclosed you will find some of my brochure, that explains the practical uses of **Clinical Hypnotherapy**.

It is difficult to refer patients to a therapist that you do not know, so I propose that we could meet to discuss my proposal in greater depth. Feel free to contact me to arrange a time when we could talk. I appreciate that there are many therapists that would like to enter into this type of arrangement with your practice. However, you must have confidence in the therapist that you are referring your patients to. I believe that you can place that confidence in me.

I look forward to speaking to you in the near future

Yours sincerely
Dr. Shaun Brookhouse

Senior Clinician, National Council for Hypnotherapy

Board Certified Hypnotherapist, Certified Instructor of Hypnotherapy, UKCP Registered Hypno-Psychotherapist
VAT Number: 727173726

Resources

Shaun's practice website: www.hypno-nlp.com

Fiona's practice website: www.fionabiddle.co.uk

The UK Academy of Therapeutic Arts and Sciences website:
www.ukacademy.org

Insurance. For home contents insurance for home based practitioners contact SMG on 0113 294 4000

Websites: for a special deal on a full website package (including Domain Registration, hosting, web design and e-mail), contact Derek Penman of Learntech
    t. 01324 878494
    f. 01324 878494
    m. 07812 334 735
    email: derek.penman@learntech.co.uk

Index

Printed in the United Kingdom by
Lightning Source UK Ltd., Milton Keynes
140175UK00001B/10/A